SKEPTICISM AND NATURALISM

WOODBRIDGE LECTURES
DELIVERED AT COLUMBIA UNIVERSITY
IN APRIL OF 1983

NUMBER TWELVE

SKEPTICISM AND NATURALISM: SOME VARIETIES

THE WOODBRIDGE LECTURES 1983

P. F. Strawson

COLUMBIA UNIVERSITY PRESS
NEW YORK 1985

B
8 37
.586
1985

Library of Congress Cataloging in Publication Data

Strawson, P. F.
  Skepticism and naturalism.

(Woodbridge lectures; no. 12)
  "The Woodbridge lectures 1983."
  Includes bibliographical references and index.
    1. Skepticism—Addresses, essays, lectures.
  2. Naturalism—Addresses, essays, lectures. I. Title.
II. Series.
B837.S86 1985   146   84-12659
ISBN 0-231-05916-7 (alk. paper)

Columbia University Press
New York
Copyright © 1985 by P. F. Strawson
All rights reserved

Printed in the United States of America

Clothbound editions of Columbia University Press Books are Smyth-sewn
and printed on permanent and durable acid-free paper

Contents

Preface

This book consists of five of the Woodbridge Lectures delivered at Columbia University in 1983. A sixth lecture, "Causation and Explanation," somewhat remote in theme and treatment from the others is not included. I wish to thank the members of the philosophy department at Columbia for their invitation to deliver these lectures and for the pleasure and stimulus of their company and comments during my stay in New York.

The lectures were originally composed in Oxford during the early months of 1980 and were subsequently delivered in that University. Though a good many of the thoughts they contain have been given, sometimes fuller, sometimes abbreviated, expression in others of my articles and reviews, they have not before been brought together and presented in print in their present form. The original composition of the lectures was prompted by a growing sense of a certain unity in the approaches, which I found plausible or appealing, to several apparently disparate topics; and by a hope, no doubt delusive, that some persistent philosophical tensions might be eased by an exposure of the parallels and connections between these approaches.

Other disciplines are defined by constitutive principles of selection among ascertainable truths. Agreement among experts in the special sciences and in exact scholarship may reasonably be hoped for and gradually attained. But philosophy, which takes human thought in general as its field, is not thus conveniently confined; and truth in philosophy, though not to be despaired of, is so complex and many-sided, so multi-faced, that any individual philosopher's work, if it is to have any unity and coherence, must at best emphasize some aspects of the truth, to the neglect of others which may strike another philosopher with greater force. Hence the appearance of endemic disagreement in the subject is something to be expected rather than deplored; and it is no matter for wonder that the individual philosopher's views are more likely than those of the scientist or exact scholar to reflect in part his individual taste and temperament.

SKEPTICISM AND NATURALISM

The satirist may laugh, the philosopher may preach; but reason herself will respect the prejudices and habits, which have been consecrated by the experience of mankind.—GIBBON

1.

Skepticism, Naturalism and Transcendental Arguments

1. INTRODUCTORY REMARKS

The term "naturalism" is elastic in its use. The fact that it has been applied to the work of philosophers having as little in common as Hume and Spinoza is enough to suggest that there is a distinction to be drawn between varieties of naturalism. In later chapters, I shall myself draw a distinction between two main varieties, within which there are subvarieties. Of the two main varieties, one might be called *strict* or *reductive* naturalism (or, perhaps, *hard* naturalism). The other might be called *catholic* or *liberal* naturalism (or, perhaps, *soft* naturalism). The words "catholic" and "liberal" I use here in their comprehensive, not in their specifically religious or political, senses; nothing I say will have any direct bearing on religion or the philosophy of religion or on politics or political philosophy.

Each of these two general varieties of naturalism will be seen by its critics as liable to lead its adherents into intellectual aberration. The exponent of some subvarieties of strict or reductive naturalism is liable to be accused of what is pejoratively known as scientism, and of denying evident truths and realities. The soft or catholic naturalist, on the other hand, is liable to be accused of fostering illusions or propagating *myths*. I do not want to suggest that a kind of intellectual cold war between the two is inevitable. There is, perhaps, a possibility of compromise or détente, even of reconciliation. The soft or catholic naturalist, as his name suggests, will be the readier with proposals for peaceful coexistence.

My title seems to speak of varieties of skepticism as well as varieties of naturalism. An exponent of some subvariety of reductive naturalism in some particular area of debate may sometimes be seen, or represented, as a kind of skeptic in that area: say, a moral skeptic or a skeptic about the mental or about abstract entities or about what are called "intensions." I shall explore some of these areas later on; and it is only then that the distinction between hard and soft naturalism will come into play.

For the present, I shall not need any such distinction and I shall not make any such slightly deviant or extended applications of the notion of skepticism. To begin with, I shall refer only to some familiar and standard forms of philosophical skepticism. Strictly, skepticism is a matter of doubt rather than of denial. The skeptic is, strictly, not one who denies the validity of certain types of belief, but one who questions, if only initially and for methodological reasons, the adequacy of our grounds for holding them. He puts forward his doubts by way of a challenge—sometimes a challenge to himself—to show that the doubts are unjustified, that the beliefs put in question are justified. He may conclude, like Descartes, that the challenge can successfully be met; or, like Hume, that it cannot (though this view of Hume's was importantly qualified). Traditional targets of philosophic doubt include the existence of the external world, i.e. of physical objects or bodies; our knowledge of other minds; the justification of induction; the reality of the past. Hume concerned himself most with the first and third of these—body and induction; and I shall refer mainly, though not only, to the first. I shall begin by considering various different kinds of attempts to meet the challenge of traditional skepticism by argument; and also various replies to these attempts, designed to show that they are unsuccessful or that they miss the point. Then I shall consider a different kind of response to skepticism—a response which does not so much attempt to meet the challenge as to pass it by. And this is where I shall first introduce an undifferentiated notion of Naturalism. The hero of this part of the story is Hume: he appears in the double role of arch-skeptic and arch-naturalist. Other names which will figure in the story include those of Moore, Wittgenstein, Carnap and, among our own contemporaries, Professor Barry Stroud. This part of the story is the theme of the present chapter. It is an old story, so I shall begin by going over some familiar ground. In the remaining chapters I shall tackle a number of different topics—viz. morality, perception, mind and meaning—and it is only in connection with these that I shall introduce and make use of the distinction between hard and soft naturalism.

2. TRADITIONAL SKEPTICISM

To begin, then, with G. E. Moore. It will be remembered that in his famous A *Defence of Common Sense*[1] Moore asserted that he, and very many other people as well, knew with certainty a

---

1. In J. H. Muirhead, ed. *Contemporary British Philosophy* (2d series) (London: Allen and Unwin, 1925; reprinted in G. E. Moore, *Philosophical Papers* (London: Allen and Unwin, 1959).

number of propositions regarding which some philosophers had held that they were not, and could not be, known with certainty. These propositions included the proposition that the earth had existed for a great many years; that on it there had been, and were now, many bodies, or physical objects, of many different kinds; that these bodies included the bodies of human beings who, like Moore himself, had had, or were having, thoughts and feelings and experiences of many different kinds. If Moore was right in holding that such propositions are widely known, with certainty, to be true, then it seems to follow that certain theses of philosophical skepticism are false: e.g. the thesis that it cannot be know with certainty that material objects exist, and the thesis that no one can know with certainty of the existence of any minds other than his own or, to put it a little more bluntly, that no one can know with certainty that there are other people. Again, the first of these two skeptical theses is implicitly challenged, indeed denied, by Moore in yet another famous paper called *Proof of an External World.*[2] He claimed, in delivering this paper, to prove that two human hands exist, hence that external things exist, by holding up first one hand, then another and saying, as he did so, "Here is one hand and here is another." The proof was rigorous and conclusive, he claimed, since he knew for certain that the premise was true and it was certain that the conclusion followed from the premise.

It was hardly to be expected that Moore's "Defence" or his "Proof" would be universally accepted as settling the questions to which they were addressed. Rather, it was felt by some philosophers that the point of philosophical skepticism about, say,

2. *Proceedings of the British Academy* (1939), vol. 25; reprinted in Moore, *Philosophical Papers.*

the existence of external things, of the physical world, was somehow being missed. A recent expression of this feeling is given by Professor Barry Stroud in an article called "The Significance of Scepticism."[3] At its most general, the skeptical point concerning the external world seems to be that subjective experience could, logically, be just the way it is without its being the case that physical or material things actually existed. (Thus Berkeley, for example, embraced a different hypothesis—that of a benevolent deity as the cause of sense-experiences—and we can find in Descartes the suggestion, though not, of course, the endorsement, of another—that of a malignant demon; while the consistent phenomenalist questions the need for any external source of sense-experience at all.) So if Moore, in making the claims he made, was simply relying on his own experience being just the way it was, he was missing the skeptical point altogether; and if he was not, then, since he issues his knowledge-claims without any further argument, all he has done is simply to issue a dogmatic denial of the skeptical thesis. But simple dogmatism settles nothing in philosophy. Stroud, at the end of his article, suggests that we ought to try to find some way of *defusing* skepticism. He does not mean, some way of establishing or proving that we do know for certain what the skeptic denies we know for certain, for he does not appear to think that this is possible; but, rather, some way of *neutralizing* the skeptical question, rendering it philosophically *impotent*. These expressions are not very clear, but I doubt if Stroud intended them to be.

Stroud mentions one attempt to neutralize the skeptical ques-

3. In P. Bieri, R. P. Horstmann, and L. Kruger, eds., *Transcendental Arguments and Science* (Reidel, 1979).

tion, an attempt which he finds unsatisfactory. The attempt is Carnap's.[4] Carnap distinguished two ways in which the words "There are or exist external or physical things" might be taken. On one interpretation these words simply express a proposition which is an obvious truism, a trivial consequence of hosts of propositions, like Moore's "Here are two hands," which are ordinarily taken, and in a sense correctly taken, to be empirically verified, to be established by and in sense-experience. On this interpretation, Moore's procedure is perfectly in order. Nevertheless Carnap would agree with Stroud that Moore's procedure is powerless to answer the *philosophical* question whether there really are physical things, powerless to establish the *philosophical* proposition that there really are such things. For Carnap accepts the point that, as the skeptic understands, or, more precisely, as he claims to understand, the words "There exist physical things," Moore's experience, or any experience, could be just the way it is without these words expressing a truth; and hence that no course of experience could establish the proposition these words are taken by the skeptic to express; that it is in principle unverifiable in experience. But the conclusion that Carnap draws is not the skeptical conclusion. The conclusion he draws is that the words, so taken, express no proposition at all; they are deprived of meaning so that the question whether the proposition they express is true or false does not arise. There is no theoretical issue here. There is indeed a practical issue: whether or not to adopt, or persist in, a certain convention, to make, or persist in, the choice of the physical-thing language or framework of concepts for the organization of experience. Given that the choice

4. Carnap, "Empiricism, Semantics and Ontology," *Revue Internationale de Philosophie* (1950), vol. 11. Reprinted in L. Linsky, ed. *Semantics and the Philosophy of Language* (Champaign: University of Illinois Press, 1952).

is made, the convention is adopted, or persisted in, then we have, internally to the adopted framework, a host of empirically verifiable thing-propositions and hence, internally to the framework, the trivial truth that there exist physical things. But the *external*, philosophical question, which the skeptic tries to raise, viz. whether the framework in general *corresponds to reality*, has no verifiable answer and hence makes no sense.

Moore, then, according to Stroud, either misses the point of the skeptical challenge or has recourse to an unacceptable dogmatism, a dogmatic claim to knowledge. Carnap, again according to Stroud, does not altogether miss the point, but seeks to smother or extinguish it by what Stroud finds an equally unacceptable verificationist dogmatism. It is all very well, says Stroud, to declare the philosophical question to be meaningless, but it does *seem* to be meaningless; the skeptical challenge, the skeptical question, *seem* to be intelligible. We should at least need more argument to be convinced that they were not.

Many philosophers would agree with Stroud, as against Carnap, on this point; and would indeed go further and contend both that the skeptical challenge is perfectly intelligible, perfectly meaningful, and that it can be met and answered by rational argument. Descartes was one such; though his appeal to the veracity of God to underwrite, or guarantee the reliability of, our natural inclination to believe in the existence of the physical world no longer seems very convincing; if it ever did. More popular today is the view that the assumption of the existence of a physical world, of physical things having more or less the characteristics and powers which our current physical theory represents them as having, provides a far better *explanation* of the course of our sensory experience than any alternative hypothesis. Such an assumption puts us in the way of a non-

arbitrary, full, detailed, coherent causal account of that experience to an extent which no alternative story comes anywhere
near rivalling. It can therefore be judged rational to accept it by
the same criteria of rationality as govern our assessment of explanatory theories framed in natural scientific enquiry or empirical inquiries generally. I shall return to this answer later.

Stroud does not discuss this approach in quite the form I have
given it; but he does discuss a near relation of it, viz. Quine's
suggestion of what he calls a "naturalised epistemology," which
would address itself to the empirical question of how, from the
meager data available to us in experience, we come to form the
elaborate structure of our ordinary and scientific beliefs about
the world.[5] Stroud acknowledges that such an enquiry is perfectly legitimate in itself; but, he contends, it leaves the skeptical
challenge completely untouched. If it were seen as an attempted
answer to the philosophical question, it would be, he main-
tains, in no better position than Moore's commonsense asser-
tion; merely a "scientific" version or analogue of the latter. We
may in the end be convinced that Quine's legitimate naturalistic
question is the only substantial one that confronts us; but if we
are to be satisfied that this is so, it must first be shown that there
is something radically faulty, radically misconceived, about the
skeptical challenge, about regarding what Carnap called the external question as raising a genuine issue. But this, says Stroud,
has not so far been shown, either by Carnap, though he asserted
it, or anyone else.

It is at this point that Stroud acknowledges the appeal of a
kind of argument which he calls "transcendental." Such arguments typically take one of two forms. A philosopher who ad-

---

5. N. V. Quine, "Epistemology Naturalized," in *Ontological Relativity* (New York:
Columbia University Press, 1969); see also *The Roots of Reference* (LaSalle, Ill.: Open
Court, 1973).

vances such an argument may begin with a premise which the skeptic does not challenge, viz. the occurrence of self-conscious thought and experience; and then proceed to argue that a necessary condition of the possibility of such experience is, say, knowledge of the existence of external objects or of states of mind of other beings. Or he may argue that the skeptic could not even raise his doubt unless he knew it to be unfounded; i.e. he could have no use for the concepts in terms of which he expresses his doubt unless he were able to know to be true at least some of the propositions belonging to the class all members of which fall within the scope of the skeptical doubt. Stroud remains dubious of the success of such arguments; presumably for the same reasons as he expounded in an earlier article entitled "Transcendental Arguments."[6] There he confronts the propounder of such arguments with a dilemma. *Either* these arguments, in their second form, are little more than an elaborate and superfluous screen behind which we can discern a simple reliance on a simple form of verification principle *or* the most that such arguments can establish is that in order for the intelligible formulation of skeptical doubts to be possible or, generally, in order for self-conscious thought and experience to be possible, we must take it, or *believe*, that we have knowledge of, say, external physical objects or other minds; but to establish this falls short of establishing that these beliefs are, or must be, true.

The second horn of the dilemma is perhaps the more attractive in that it at least allows that transcendental argument may demonstrate something about the use and interconnection of our concepts. But if the dilemma is sound, the skeptic's withers are unwrung in any case. (Stroud seems to assume without question

6. *Journal of Philosophy*, 1968; reprinted in T. Penelham and J. J. MacIntosh, eds. *The First Critique* (Belmont: Wadsworth, 1969) and in Walker, ed., *Kant on Pure Reason* (Oxford: Oxford University Press, 1982).

that the point of transcendental argument in general is an anti-skeptical point; but the assumption may be questioned, as I shall later suggest. In either case, according to Stroud, the skeptic is unshaken because he does not deny that we do, and need not deny that we must, employ and apply the concepts in question in experiential conditions which we take to warrant or justify their application. His point is, and remains, that the fulfillment of those conditions is consistent with the falsity of all the propositions we then affirm; and hence that—failing further argument to the contrary—we cannot be said really to *know* that any such propositions are true.

3. HUME: REASON AND NATURE

Is there any other way with skepticism which is not a variant on those I have referred to, i.e. is neither an attempt directly to refute it by rational argument drawing on commonsense or theological or quasi-scientific considerations nor an attempt indirectly to refute it by showing that it is in some way unintelligible or self-defeating? I think there is another way. There is nothing new about it, since it is at least as old as Hume; and the most powerful latter-day exponent of a closely related position is Wittgenstein. I shall call it the way of Naturalism; though this name is not to be understood in the sense of Quine's "naturalised epistemology."

In a famous sentence in Book II of the *Treatise* Hume limits the pretensions of reason to determine the ends of action.[7] In a similar spirit, towards the end of Book I, he limits the pretensions of reason to determine the formation of beliefs concerning

---

7. "Reason is and ought only to be the slave of the passions and can never pretend to any other office than to serve and obey them." *Treatise of Human Nature*, Selby-Bigge, ed., bk. 2, sec. 3, p. 415.

matters of fact and existence. He points out that all arguments in *support* of the skeptical position are totally inefficacious; and, by the same token, all arguments *against* it are totally idle. His point is really the very simple one that, whatever arguments may be produced on one side or the other of the question, we simply *cannot help* believing in the existence of body, and *cannot help* forming beliefs and expectations in general accordance with the basic canons of induction. He might have added, though he did not discuss this question, that the belief in the existence of other people (hence other minds) is equally inescapable. Hume regularly expresses his point by reference to Nature, which leaves us no option in these matters but "by absolute and uncontrollable necessity" determines us "to judge as well as to breathe and feel." Speaking of that total skepticism which, arguing from the fallibility of human judgment, would tend to undermine all belief and opinion, he says: "Whoever has taken the pains to refute the cavils of this total scepticism has really disputed without an antagonist and endeavoured by arguments to establish a faculty which Nature has antecedently implanted in the mind and rendered unavoidable."[8] He goes on to point out that what holds for total skepticism holds also for skepticism about the existence of body. Even the professed skeptic *"must assent* to the principle concerning the existence of body, though he cannot pretend by any arguments of philosophy to maintain its veracity"; for "nature has not left this to his choice, and has doubtless esteemed it an affair of too great importance to be entrusted to our uncertain reasonings and speculations." Hence " 'tis vain to ask Whether there be body or not? That is a point which we must take for granted in all our reasonings."[9]

Here I interpolate some remarks which are not strictly to the

8. *Ibid.*, p. 183.
9. *Ibid.*, p. 187.

present purpose but which are very much to the purpose if one is considering the question of Hume himself. Hume contrasts the vain question, *Whether there be body or not?* with a question he says "we may well ask," viz. *What causes induce us to believe in the existence of body?*—thus seeming to anticipate Quine's program for a naturalized epistemology. But there follows, in Hume, what seems to be a striking inconsistency between principle and practice. For, having said that the existence of body is a point which we must take for granted in *all* our reasonings, he then conspicuously does *not* take it for granted in the reasonings which he addresses to the causal question. Indeed those reasonings famously point to a skeptical conclusion. So, as he himself is the first to acknowledge,[10] there is an unresolved tension in Hume's position (a tension which may be found reminiscent in some ways of the tension between Kant's empirical realism and his transcendental idealism). One might speak of two Humes: Hume the skeptic and Hume the naturalist; where Hume's naturalism, as illustrated by the passages I quoted, appears as something like a refuge from his skepticism. An exponent of a more thoroughgoing naturalism could accept the question, *What causes induce us to believe in the existence of body?* as one we may well ask, as one that can be referred to empirical psychology, to the study of infantile development; but would do so in the justified expectation that answers to it would in fact take for granted the existence of body.

Hume, then, we may say, is ready to accept and to tolerate a distinction between two levels of thought: the level of philosophically critical thinking which can offer us no assurances against skepticism; and the level of everyday empirical thinking,

---

10. *Ibid.*, Bk. 1, pt. 4, sec 7, *passim.*

at which the pretensions of critical thinking are completely overridden and suppressed by Nature, by an inescapable natural commitment to belief: to belief in the existence of body and in inductively based expectations. (I hinted at a parallel with Kant; and a parallel there is, though it is only a loose one. There is a parallel in that Kant also recognizes two levels of thought: the empirical level at which we justifiably claim knowledge of an external world of causally related objects in space; and the critical level at which we recognize that this world is only appearance, appearance of an ultimate reality of which we can have no positive knowledge at all. The parallel, however, is only a loose one. Where Hume refers to an inescapable *natural disposition* to belief, Kant produces *argument* [transcendental argument] to show that what, at the empirical level, is rightly reckoned as empirical knowledge of an external world of law-governed objects is a necessary condition of self-awareness, of knowledge of our own inner states; and—a yet more striking difference—where, at the critical level, Hume leaves us with unrefuted skepticism, Kant offers us his own brand of idealism.)

Here I end my digression concerning the complex tensions in Hume's thought and the parallels with Kant; and return to a consideration of Hume as naturalist, leaving on one side Hume the skeptic. According to Hume the naturalist, skeptical doubts are not to be met by argument. They are simply to be neglected (except, perhaps, in so far as they supply a harmless amusement, a mild diversion to the intellect). They are to be neglected because they are *idle*; powerless against the force of nature, of our naturally implanted disposition to belief. This does not mean that Reason has no part to play in relation to our beliefs concerning matters of fact and existence. It has a part to play, though a subordinate one: as Nature's lieutenant rather than

Nature's commander. (Here we may recall and adapt that famous remark about Reason and the passions.) Our inescapable natural commitment is to a general frame of belief and to a general style (the inductive) of belief-formation. But *within* that frame and style, the requirement of Reason, that our beliefs should form a consistent and coherent system, may be given full play. Thus, for example, though Hume did not think that a rational justification of induction in general was either necessary or possible, he could quite consistently proceed to frame "rules for judging of cause and effect." Though it is Nature which commits us to inductive belief-formation in general, it is Reason which leads us to refine and elaborate our inductive canons and procedures and, in their light, to criticize, and sometimes to reject, what in detail we find ourselves naturally inclined to believe.

4. HUME AND WITTGENSTEIN

In introducing this way with skepticism, I associated the name of Wittgenstein with that of Hume. I have in mind primarily Wittgenstein's notes *On Certainty*.[11] Like Hume, Wittgenstein distinguishes between those matters—those propositions—which are up for question and decision in the light of reason and experience and those which are not, which are, as he puts it, "exempt from doubt." Of course there are differences between Hume and Wittgenstein. We do not, for example, find in Wittgenstein any explicit repetition of Hume's quite explicit appeal to Nature. But, as we shall see, the resemblances, and even the echoes, are more striking than the differences. Above all, there is, in Wittgenstein's work, as in Hume's, the distinction between "what

11. Wittgenstein, *On Certainty* (Oxford: Basil Blackwell, 1969).

it is vain" to make a matter of inquiry, what "we must take for granted in all our reasonings," as Hume puts it, on the one hand, and what is genuinely matter for inquiry on the other. Wittgenstein has a host of phrases to express this antithesis. Thus he speaks of a kind of conviction or belief as "*beyond being justified or unjustified*; as it were, as something *animal*" (359);[12] and here we may find an echo of Hume's appeal to Nature and, even more, of Hume's remark that "belief is more properly an act of the sensitive than of the cogitative part of our nature."[13] Again, Wittgenstein says that "certain propositions seem to *underlie* all questions and all thinking" (415); that "some propositions are *exempt from doubt*" (341); that "certain things are *in deed* [in der Tat, in practice] not doubted" (342); he speaks of "belief that is not founded" (253) but "in the entire system of our language-games *belongs to the foundations*" (411). Again, he speaks of "propositions which have *a peculiar logical role* in the system [of our empirical propositions]" (136); which belong to our "*frame of reference*" (83); which "*stand fast or solid*" (151); which constitute the "world-picture" which is "the *substratum* of all my enquiring and asserting" (162) or "the *scaffolding* of our thoughts" (211) or "the element in which arguments have their life" (105). This world-picture, he says, is not something he has because he has satisfied himself of its correctness. "No: it is the inherited background against which I distinguish between true and false" (94). He compares the propositions de-

---

12. Each quoted phrase is followed by its paragraph number in the text of *On Certainty*. Italics are generally mine.

13. *Treatise*, bk. 1, pt. 4, sec. 1, p. 183. another Humean echo is found at para. 135: "But we do not simply follow the principle that what has always happened will happen again (or something like it)? What does it mean to follow this principle? Do we really *introduce* it into our reasoning? Or is it merely the *natural law* which our inferring apparently follows? This latter it may be. It is not an item in our considerations."

scribing this world-picture to the rules of a game which "can be learned purely practically without learning any explicit rules" (95). Though the general tendency of Wittgenstein's position is clear enough, it is not easy to extract a wholly clear consecutive statement of it from the mass of figures or metaphors which I have illustrated. Evidently his aim, at least in part, is to give a realistic account or description of how it actually is with our human systems or bodies of belief. Evidently, too, he distinguishes, as I have said, between those propositions, or actual or potential elements in our belief-systems, which we treat as subject to empirical confirmation or falsification, which we consciously incorporate in our belief-system (when we do) for this or that *reason* or on the basis of this or that *experience*, or which we actually treat as matter for inquiry or doubt—and, on the other hand, those elements of our belief-system which have a quite different character, alluded to by the figures of scaffolding, framework, background, substratum, etc. (The metaphors include that of foundations; but it is quite clear that Wittgenstein does not regard these propositions, or elements of the belief-system, as foundations in the traditional empiricist sense, i.e. as basic reasons, themselves resting on experience, for the rest of our beliefs. The metaphor of a scaffolding or framework, within which the activity of building or modifying the structure of our beliefs goes on, is a better one.)

Wittgenstein does not represent this distinction between two kinds of element in our belief-systems as sharp, absolute, and unchangeable. On the contrary. And this is just as well in view of some of his examples of propositions of the second class, i.e. of propositions which are "exempt from doubt." (Writing in 1950–51, he gives as one example the proposition that no one has been very far [e.g. as far as the moon] from the surface of the earth.)

It would have been helpful, though probably contrary to his inclinations, if he had drawn distinctions, or indicated a *principle* of distinction, *within* this class. An indication that there are such distinctions to be drawn comes at the end of an extended metaphor (96–99) in which he compares those propositions which are subject to empirical test to the waters moving in a river and those which are not so subject to the bed or banks of the river. The situation is not unchangeable in that there may sometimes be shifts of the bed or even of the bank. But, he concludes, "The bank of that river consists partly of hard rock, *subject to no alteration or only to an imperceptible one,* partly of sand which now in one place now in another gets washed away or deposited."

But how close, really, is Wittgenstein to Hume? There are points at which he may seem closer to Carnap. These are the points at which he seems disposed to express his sense of the difference between those propositions which are subject to empirical test and those which form the scaffolding, framework, foundations etc. of our thought (the hard rock of the river bank) by denying to the latter the status of propositions at all—comparing them, as we have seen, to rules "which can be learned purely practically." Thus he writes at one point: "No such proposition as 'There are physical objects' can be formulated" (36); and even that " 'There are physical objects' is nonsense" (35). But he is not very close to Carnap. Carnap speaks of a practical issue, a choice—a decision to adopt, or to persist in the use of, a certain framework. There is nothing of this in Wittgenstein. "It is not," he says, "as if we *chose* the game" (317). And elsewhere, though he is dissatisfied with the expression, we find: "I want to say: propositions of the form of empirical propositions, and not only propositions of logic, form the foundation of all operating with thoughts (with language)" (401). (There is here an evident allusion to the *Tractatus*.) Later, straightforwardly enough, we find: "certain propositions seem to underlie all questions and all thinking." The apparent shilly-shallying over "proposition" is perhaps palliated by the remarks at 319–20, where he speaks of a lack of sharpness in the boundary between rule and empirical proposition and adds that the concept 'proposition' is itself not a sharp one.[14]

To sum up now the relations between Hume and Wittgenstein. Hume's position seems much the simpler. All that is explicitly mentioned by him as constituting the framework of all inquiry—what is to be "taken for granted in all our reasoning"—amounts to two things: acceptance of the existence of body and of the general reliability of inductive belief-formation. This is the groundwork; and its source is unambiguously identified. These unavoidable natural convictions, commitments, or prejudices are ineradicably implanted in our minds by Nature. Wittgenstein's position is, as we have seen, at least superficially more complicated. First, the propositions or crypto-propositions of the framework, though they may be taken to include the two Humean elements, are presumptively more various. Second, the framework is, up to a point at least, dynamically conceived: what was at one time part of the framework may change its status, may assume the character of a hypothesis to be questioned and perhaps falsified—some of what we would now regard as assumptions about supernatural agents or powers presumably come

14. The restrictions which Wittgenstein is conspicuously inclined to place on the concept of knowledge, on the use of the verb "to know," reflect, and more emphatically, the inclination to restrict the application of the concept of a proposition. Only what are clearly propositions subject to empirical testing are, he consistently implies, proper objects of the verb "to know"; just as only they can be genuinely objects of doubt.

into this category—whereas other parts of the framework remain fixed and unalterable. Finally, and connectedly, Wittgenstein does not speak, as Hume does, of one exclusive source, viz. Nature, for these *préjugés*. Rather, he speaks of our learning, from childhood up, an activity, a practice, a social practice—of making judgements, of forming beliefs—to which the crypto-propositions have the special relation he seeks to illuminate by the figures of framework, scaffolding, substratum etc.; that is, they are not judgments we actually make or, in general, things we explicitly learn or are taught in the course of that practice, but rather reflect the general character of the practice itself, form a frame within which the judgments we actually make hang together in a more or less coherent way.

In spite of the greater complication of Wittgenstein's position, we can, I think, at least as far as the general skeptical questions are concerned, discern a profound community between him and Hume. They have in common the view that our "beliefs" in the existence of body and, to speak roughly, in the general reliability of induction are not grounded beliefs and at the same time are not open to serious doubt. They are, one might say, outside our critical and rational competence in the sense that they define, or help to define, the area in which that competence is exercised. To attempt to confront the professional skeptical doubt with arguments in support of these beliefs, with rational justifications, is simply to show a total misunderstanding of the role they actually play in our belief-systems. The correct way with the professional skeptical doubt is not to attempt to rebut it with argument, but to point out that it is idle, unreal, a pretense; and then the rebutting arguments will appear as equally idle; the reasons produced in those arguments to justify induction or belief in the existence of body are not, and do not become, *our* reasons for these beliefs; there is no such thing as *the reasons for which we hold* these beliefs. We simply cannot help accepting them as defining the areas within which the questions come up of what beliefs we should rationally hold on such-and-such a matter. The point may be underlined by referring again to some attempts to rebut skepticism by argument.

Perhaps the best skepticism-rebutting argument in favor of the existence of body is the quasi-scientific argument I mentioned earlier: i.e., that the existence of a world of physical objects having more or less the properties which current science attributes to them provides the best available explanation of the phenomena of experience, just as accepted theories within physical science supply the best available explanations of the physical phenomena they deal with. But the implicit comparison with scientific theory simply proclaims its own weakness. We accept or believe the scientific theories (when we do) just because we believe they supply the best available explanations of the phenomena they deal with. That is our reason for accepting them. But no one accepts the existence of the physical world *because* it supplies the best available explanation etc. That is no one's reason for accepting it. Anyone who claimed it was his reason would be pretending. It is, as Hume declared, a point we are naturally bound to take for granted in all our reasonings and, in particular, in all those reasonings which underlie our acceptance of particular physical theories.

Similarly, the best argument against other-minds skepticism is, probably, that, given the non-uniqueness of one's physical constitution and the general uniformity of nature in the biological sphere as in others, it is in the highest degree improbable that one is unique among members of one's species in being the enjoyer of subjective states, and of the kind of subjective states one does enjoy in the kind of circumstances in which one enjoys them. But, again, this is no one's reason for believing in the existence of other minds, of other people, subjects of just such a range of sensations, emotions, and thoughts as he is aware of in himself. We simply react to others as to other *people*. They may puzzle us at times; but that is part of so reacting. Here again we have something which we have no option but to take for granted in all our reasoning.

5. "ONLY CONNECT": THE ROLE OF TRANSCENDENTAL ARGUMENTS

Suppose we accept this naturalist rejection both of skepticism and of skepticism-rebutting arguments as equally idle—as both involving a misunderstanding of the role in our lives, the place in our intellectual economy, of those propositions or crypto-propositions which the skeptic seeks to place in doubt and his opponent in argument seeks to establish. How, in this perspective, should we view arguments of the kind which Stroud calls "transcendental"? Evidently not as supplying the reasoned rebuttal which the skeptic perversely invites. Our naturalism is precisely the rejection of that invitation. So, even if we have a tenderness for transcendental arguments, we shall be happy to accept the criticism of Stroud and others that either such arguments rely on an unacceptably simple verificationism or the most they can establish is a certain sort of interdependence of conceptual capacities and beliefs: e.g., as I put it earlier, that in order for the intelligible formulation of skeptical doubts to be possible or, more generally, in or order for self-conscious thought and experience to be possible, we must take it, or *believe*, that we have knowledge of external physical objects or other minds. The fact that such a demonstration of dependence would not refute the skeptic does not worry our naturalist, who repudiates any such aim. But our naturalist might well take satisfaction in the demonstration of these connections—if they can indeed be demonstrated—for their own sake. For repudiation of the project of wholesale validation of types of knowledge-claim does not leave the naturalist without philosophical employment. E. M. Forster's motto—"only connect"—is as valid for the naturalist at the philosophical level as it is for Forster's characters (and us) at the moral and personal level. That is to say, having given up the unreal project of wholesale validation, the naturalist philosopher will embrace the real project of investigating the connections between the major structural elements of our conceptual scheme. If connections as tight as those which transcendental arguments, construed as above, claim to offer are really available, so much the better.

Of course, it is often disputed, both in detail and in general, that arguments of this kind do or can achieve even as much as the most that Stroud allowed them. Typically, a transcendental argument, as now construed, claims that one type of exercise of conceptual capacity is a necessary condition of another (e.g. that taking some experiences to consist in awareness of objects in physical space is a necessary condition of the self-ascription of subjective states as ordered in time or that being equipped to identify some states of mind in others is a necessary condition of being able to ascribe any states of mind to ourselves). I am not now concerned with the question of the validity of such arguments but with the general character of the criticisms to which they are typically subject. Typically, the criticism is that what is claimed to be a necessary condition has not been shown to be so and could not be shown to be so without eliminating all possible (or candidate) alternatives, a task which is not attempted. The transcendental arguer is always exposed to the charge that even if *he* cannot conceive of alternative ways in which conditions of the possibility of a certain kind of experience or exercise of conceptual capacity might be fulfilled, this inability may simply be due to lack of imagination on his part—a lack which makes him prone to mistake sufficient for necessary conditions.

It is not my present purpose to inquire how successfully arguments of the kind in question (on the present relatively modest construal of their aims) survive these criticisms; to inquire, that is, whether some or any of them are strictly valid. I am inclined to think that at least some are (e.g. self-ascription implies the capacity for other-ascription), though I must admit that few, if any, have commanded universal assent among the critics. But whether or not they are strictly valid, these arguments, or weakened versions of them, will continue to be of interest to our naturalist philosopher. For even if they do not succeed in establishing such tight or rigid connections as they initially promise, they do at least indicate or bring out conceptual connections, even if only of a looser kind; and, as I have already suggested, to establish the connections between the major structural features or elements of our conceptual scheme—to exhibit it, not as a rigidly deductive system, but as a coherent whole whose parts are mutually supportive and mutually dependent, interlocking in an intelligible way—to do this may well seem to our naturalist the proper, or at least the major, task of analytical philosophy. As indeed it does to me. (Whence the phrase, "descriptive [as opposed to validatory or revisionary] metaphysics.")

6. THREE QUOTATIONS

Vis-à-vis traditional skepticism, then, I am proposing that we adopt, at least provisionally (and everything in philosophy is provisional), the naturalist position. Or, perhaps, since we have yoked Wittgenstein to Hume in characterizing and illustrating the position, we should qualify the name and, since where Hume speaks only of Nature, Wittgenstein speaks of the language-games we learn from childhood up, i.e. in a social context, should call it, not simply 'naturalism', but 'social naturalism'. Whatever the name, I can perhaps illustrate the break that adoption of it constitutes with other attitudes with the help of two quotations: the first from the greatest of modern philosophers, the second from a philosopher whose title to respect is less considerable, but who nevertheless seems to me to be on the right side on this point.

In the Preface to the second edition of *The Critique of Pure Reason* (B xi) Kant says: "it remains a scandal to philosophy and to human reason in general that the existence of things outside us . . . must be accepted merely on *faith* and that if anyone thinks good to doubt their existence, we are unable to counter his doubts by any satisfactory proof."

In *Being and Time* (I. 6) Heidegger ripostes: "The 'scandal of philosophy' is not that this proof has yet to be given, but that *such proofs are expected and attempted again and again.*"

To complete this short series of quotations, here is one, from Wittgenstein again, that neatly sums things up from the naturalist, or social naturalist, point of view: "It is so difficult to find the *beginning.* Or better: it is difficult to begin at the beginning. And not to try to go further back." (471)

To try to meet the skeptic's challenge, in whatever way, by whatever style of argument, is to try to go further back. If one is to begin at the beginning, one must refuse the challenge as our naturalist refuses it.

7. HISTORICISM: AND THE PAST

But now, as Wittgenstein's first thought—as opposed to what he calls the better thought—in that quotation suggests, the question arises: Where exactly is the beginning? In other words, what are those structural features of our conceptual scheme, the framework features, which must be regarded as equally beyond question and beyond validation, but which offer themselves, rather, for the kind of philosophical treatment which I have suggested and which might be called "connective analysis"? Hume, in Book I of the *Treatise*, concentrates, as we saw, on two such features: the habit of induction and the belief in the existence of body, of the physical world. Wittgenstein seems to offer, or suggest, a more miscellaneous collection, though he mitigates the miscellaneousness by the dynamic element in his picture, the provision for change: some things which at some time, or in some context or relation, may have the status of framework features, beyond question or test, may at another time, or in another context or relation, become open to question or even be rejected; others are fixed and unalterable. Part, though not the whole, of the explanation of what may seem cloudy or unsatisfactory in Wittgenstein's treatment in *On Certainty* is that he is fighting on more than one front. He is not concerned only with the common framework of human belief-systems at large. He is also concerned to indicate what a realistic picture of *individual* belief-systems is like; and in such a picture room must be found for, as it were, local and idiosyncratic propositions (like "My name is Ludwig Wittgenstein") as elements in someone's belief-system which are, for him, neither grounded nor up for question. But, obviously, no such proposition as that forms part of the common framework of human belief-systems at large.

But now it might be suggested that—even setting aside the point about individual belief-systems—Wittgenstein's admission of a dynamic element in the *collective* belief-system puts the whole approach in question. Earlier on, the unfortunate example, of the conviction that no one has been as far from the surface of the earth as the moon, was mentioned. One can think of more far-reaching beliefs. Surely the geocentric view of the universe—or at least of what we now call the solar system—at one time formed part of the framework of human thinking at large. Or, again, some form of creation-myth. Or some form of animism. If our "frame of reference," to use Wittgenstein's phrase, can undergo such radical revolutions as the Copernican (the real, not the Kantian, Copernican revolution), why should we assume that anything in it is "fixed and unalterable"? And if we drop that assumption, must we not be content to cast our metaphysics for a more modest—a historical or historicist—role; somewhat in the spirit of Collingwood,[15] who declared that metaphysics was indeed an essentially historical study, the attempt to elicit what he called the "absolute presuppositions" of the science of the day? Metaphysical truth would thus be relativized to historical periods. Derelativization could be achieved only by explicitly assigning a system of presuppositions to its historical place. ("At such-and-such a period it *was* absolutely presupposed that . . ." or "As of now, it *is* absolutely presupposed that . . .").

In fact, there is no reason why metaphysics should tamely

---

15. Collingwood, *An Essay on Metaphysics* (London: Oxford University Press, 1940).

submit to historicist pressure of this kind. The human world-picture is of course subject to change. But it remains a *human world-picture:* a picture of a world of physical objects (bodies) in space and time including human observers capable of action and of acquiring and imparting knowledge (and error) both of themselves and each other and of whatever else is to be found in nature. So much of a constant conception, of what, in Wittgenstein's phrase, is "not subject to alteration or only to an imperceptible one," is given along with the very idea of historical alteration in the human world-view.

It is all of a piece with Wittgenstein's extreme aversion, in his later work, from any systematic treatment of issues, that he never attempted to specify which aspects of our world-picture, our frame of reference, are "not subject to alteration or only to an imperceptible one"; to which aspects our human or natural commitment is so profound that they stand fast, and may be counted on to stand fast, through all revolutions of scientific thought or social development. So far only those aspects have been specifically mentioned, or dwelt on to any extent, which have a relevance to—or show the irrelevance of—certain traditional skeptical problems: concerning the existence of body, knowledge of other minds and the practice of induction. I shall not attempt now to compile a list, or to engage in the connective metaphysical task of exhibiting the relations and interdependences of the elements of the general structure. But, before I pass on to a different, though related, set of questions, I want to mention now one further aspect of our thought which seems to have a similarly inescapable character; and I choose it because of its relevance to some current discussions.

It is to be remembered that the point has been, not to offer a rational justification of the belief in external objects and other minds or of the practice of induction, but to represent skeptical arguments and rational counter-arguments as equally idle—not senseless, but idle—since what we have here are original, natural, inescapable commitments which we neither choose nor could give up. The further such commitment which I now suggest we should acknowledge is the commitment to belief in the reality and determinateness of the past. This is worth mentioning at the moment, not because it is a topic of traditional skeptical challenge, but because it is currently a topic of challenge from a certain kind of limited or moderate anti-realism, based on a particular, quasi-verificationist theory of meaning.[16] Of course, it *could* be a topic of skeptical challenge, a challenge, e.g., taking a form which Russell once toyed with: i.e. "We have no guarantee, no certain knowledge, that the world didn't come into existence just five minutes ago; all our current experience, including our apparent memories, could be just as it is consistently with this being the case." But the current challenge is different. Roughly speaking (some of the challengers would probably say this is a good deal too rough), it allows, with respect to questions about the past, that there is a determinate fact of the matter in those cases to which our memories or conclusively confirming or falsifying evidence extend (or it is known could be brought to extend), but no determinate fact of the matter in any other cases. Only those questions about the past which we can answer (or bring ourselves into a position to answer) *have* answers, true or false. (One casualty of this view, evidently, is standard logic—which is deprived of the law of excluded middle.) Much subtlety of argument can be devoted to advancing this view and to opposing it. But my present concern is not to

16. Cf. Michael Dummett, "The Reality of the Past," in *Truth and Other Enigmas* (London: Duckworth, 1978).

meet it with argument, but to suggest, again, that arguments on both sides are idle, since belief in the reality and determinateness of the past is as much part of that general framework of beliefs to which we are inescapably committed as is belief in the existence of physical objects and the practice of inductive belief-formation. Indeed, it would be hard to separate the conception of objects which we have and our acceptance of inductively formed beliefs from that conception of the past. All form part of our mutually supportive natural metaphysics. We are equally happy to acknowledge, with the poet, that full many a flower is born to blush unseen and, with the naturalist metaphysician, that full many a historical fact is destined to remain unverified and unverifiable by subsequent generations.

2.

Morality and Perception

1. INVOLVEMENT AND DETACHMENT

I turn now to another area of natural commitment, different from any that I have mentioned so far. It is in this new connection that the distinction between varieties of naturalism which I spoke of at the outset will, in due course, make its first appearance. The area I have in mind is that of those attitudes and feelings, or "sentiments," as we used to say, toward ourselves and others, in respect of our and their actions, which can be grouped together under the heads of moral attitudes and judgments and personal reactive attitudes and are indissolubly linked with that sense of agency or freedom or responsibility which we feel in ourselves and attribute to others. I shall not now attempt a detailed description of this cluster of phenomena since I have written about some of them fairly extensively in "Freedom and Resentment."[1] The sources of challenge to these attitudes and feelings, the sources of the ("skeptical") suggestion that they are unwarranted, inappropriate or irrational are familiar to anyone who has taken an interest in the Free Will controversy; and have

1. Strawson, *Freedom, and Resentment* (London: Methuen, 1974).

recently been admirably characterized by Professor Tom Nagel. I refer to an article called "Moral Luck"[2] and especially to its concluding paragraphs. The fundamental thought is that once we see people and their doings (including ourselves and our doings) objectively, as what they are, namely as natural objects and happenings, occurrences in the course of nature—whether causally determined occurrences or chance occurrences—then the veil of illusion cast over them by moral attitudes and reactions must, or should, slip away. What simply happens in nature may be matter for rejoicing or regret, but not for gratitude or resentment, for moral approval or blame, or for moral self-approval or remorse.

Attempts to counter such reasoning by defending the reality of some special condition of freedom or spontaneity or self-determination which human beings enjoy and which supplies a justifying ground for our moral attitudes and judgments have not been notably successful; for no one has been able to state intelligibly what such a condition of freedom, supposed to be necessary to ground our moral attitudes and judgments, would actually consist in.

Such attempts at counter-argument are misguided; and not merely because they are unsuccessful or unintelligible. They are misguided also for the reasons for which counter-arguments to other forms of skepticism have been seen to be misguided; i.e. because the arguments they are directed against are totally inefficacious. We can no more be reasoned out of our proneness to personal and moral reactive attitudes in general than we can be reasoned out of our belief in the existence of body. Of course, we can be convinced that a particular reaction of ours on a par-

2. Nagel, *Mortal Questions* (Cambridge: Cambridge University Press, 1979).

ticular occasion was unjustified, just as we can be convinced in particular cases that what we took for a physical object, or a physical object of a certain kind, was no such thing. But our *general* proneness to these attitudes and reactions is inextricably bound up with that involvement in personal and social interrelationships which begins with our lives, which develops and complicates itself in a great variety of ways throughout our lives and which is, one might say, a condition of our humanity. What we have, in our inescapable commitment to these attitudes and feelings, is a natural fact, something as deeply rooted in our natures as our existence as social beings. It is interesting that Thomas Reid, that doughty opponent of the skepticism of his fellow-Scot, David Hume, draws an explicit parallel between our natural commitment to belief in external things and our natural proneness to moral or quasi-moral response. He is careful not to suggest that the child in the womb or newly born has such a belief or proneness; at that stage he may be, as Reid puts it, "merely a sentient being"; but the belief and proneness in question are, he says, *natural* principles, implanted in his constitution, and *activated* when, as he agreeably puts it, the growing child "has occasion for them."[3] Here we see Reid aligning himself with Hume the naturalist against Hume the skeptic.

Besides its parallel with the cases previously considered and its contemporary, and indeed perennial, interest, I have another reason for mentioning this area of natural commitment. I have spoken of it as "inescapable"; and indeed I think it is unshakable by arguments which seek to cast doubt on the reality of human freedom. Nevertheless, that adjective, "inescapable," needs

3. The parallel may be found at the end of section VII of chapter 5 of Reid's *Inquiry into the Human Mind*, published in 1764 while Hume was still alive. The specific response Reid dwells on is that of resentment of injury.

qualification. For, as argued in "Freedom and Resentment," it is possible for us sometimes to achieve a kind of detachment from the whole range of natural attitudes and reactions I have been speaking of and to view another person (and even, perhaps, though this must surely be more difficult, oneself) in a purely objective light—to see another or others simply as natural creatures whose behavior, whose actions and reactions, we may seek to understand, predict and perhaps control in just such a sense as that in which we may seek to understand, predict, and control the behavior of nonpersonal objects in nature. I do not mean merely to speak of the intellectual recognition or acknowledgment, to which Nagel invites us, that people are such creatures. I mean to speak of a state in which this recognition so colors and dominates our attitudes to them as to exclude or suppress the natural personal or moral reactive attitudes. Again, I do not mean to speak only or primarily of cases in which this objectivity of attitude is more or less forced upon us, or is at least felt to be itself humanly natural, because of the extreme abnormality of the case we are presented with—as, for example, when we are confronted with someone who is quite out of his mind. I mean that there is open to us the possibility of having deliberate recourse to an objective attitude in perfectly normal cases; that it is a resource we can sometimes temporarily make use of, for reasons of policy or curiosity or emotional self-defense. I say "temporarily," because I do not think it is a point of view or position which we can hold, or rest in, for very long. The price of doing so would be higher than we are willing, or able, to pay; it would be the loss of all human involvement in personal relationships, of all fully participant social engagement.

The possibility that I here mention is, then, not a possibility which is often fully realized, even temporarily; though perhaps we all edge a little way toward it from time to time. But it is worth mentioning, both for its own sake and because it exemplifies a general notion which I shall invoke again in other connections: the notion of a radical difference in the standpoint from which what are in a sense identical objects or events or phenomena may be viewed. Viewed from one standpoint, the standpoint that we naturally occupy as social beings, human behavior appears as the proper object of all those personal and moral reactions, judgments and attitudes to which, as social beings, we are naturally prone; or, to put the same point differently, human actions and human agents appear as the bearers of objective moral properties. But if anyone consistently succeeded in viewing such behavior in what I have called the "purely objective," or what might better be called the "purely naturalistic," light, then to him such reactions, judgments, and attitudes would be alien; the notion of "proper objects" of such reactions and attitudes, the notion of "objective moral properties," would for him lack significance; rather, he would *observe* the prevalence of such reactions and attitudes in those around him, could establish correlations between types of attitude and the types of behavior which observably evoked them, and generally treat this whole range of moral and personal reaction, attitude, and judgment as yet another range of natural phenomena to be studied; to be understood, in a sense, but not in the way of understanding which involves sharing or sympathizing with. Such a position would be akin to that recommended by Spinoza—that of the "free man" in Spinoza's idiosyncratic use of the expression. I have described it in the conditional mood, i.e. have said how it would be rather than how it is, in order to emphasize the point which I began with: our human incapacity, as beings committed to participant relationships and acting under the sense of freedom, to hold such position for more than a limited period in limited connections.

At this point one may feel a strong temptation to raise, and to press, a certain question. I have spoken of two different standpoints from which human behavior may be viewed: for short, the "participant" versus the "objective," the "involved" versus the "detached." One standpoint is associated with a certain range of attitudes and reactions, the other with a different range of attitudes and reactions. Standpoints and attitudes are not only different, they are profoundly opposed. One cannot be whole-heartedly committed to both at once. It will not do to say that they are mutually exclusive; since we are rarely whole-hearted creatures. But they tend in the limit to mutual exclusion. How natural it is, then, to ask the question: "Which is the correct standpoint? Which is the standpoint from which we see things as they really are?"

One the question is asked, it is natural to go on to argue as follows: If it is the standpoint of participation and involvement, to which we are so strongly committed by nature and society, which is correct, then some human actions really are morally blameworthy or praiseworthy, hateful or admirable, proper objects of gratitude or resentment; and those who have contended for the objectivity of morals are fundamentally in the right of it, even if the particular judgments we make in this area are even more liable to error or distortion than those we make in others; and to refuse to recognize this is deliberately to blind oneself to a whole dimension of reality. If, on the other hand, it is only from the so-called "objective" standpoint that we see things as they really are, then all our moral and quasi-moral reactions and judgments, however natural they may be and however widely shared, are *no more* than natural human reactions; no question of their truth or falsity arises, for there is no moral reality for them to represent or misrepresent. They are never justified or apropriate; not because the moral facts are always different from what they are taken to be, but because there are no such things as moral facts. The idea of objective moral right or wrong, moral desert, moral good or evil, is a human illusion, as Spinoza held; or, at best, as John Mackie put it, a human invention.[4] All there is in this area is human behavior and human reactions to human behavior, both, indeed, proper objects for study and understanding; but no more.[5]

2. THE RELATIVIZING MOVE; AND THE TWO FACES OF NATURALISM

What I want now to suggest is that error lies not one side or the other of these two contrasting positions, but in the attempt to force the choice between them. The question was: From which standpoint do we see things as they really are? and it carried the implication that the answer cannot be: from both. It is this implication that I want to dispute. But surely, it may be said, two contradictory views cannot both be true; it cannot be the case *both* that there really is such a thing as moral desert *and* that there is no such thing, *both* that some human actions really are

4 Mackie, *Ethics: Inventing Right and Wrong* (London: Penguin Books, 1977).

5. Let me remark, in passing, on one popular misrepresentation, or misunderstanding, of this last position, embodied in the slogan, "Tout comprendre, c'est tout pardonner" or "To understand all is to forgive all." This is a misrepresentation of the position because forgiveness belongs precisely to the range of attitudes and reactions which, on the view currently being considered, are undermined or shown to have no proper objects if the objective standpoint is the correct one. Only where there is supposed to be genuine wrong can there be genuine forgiveness.

Incidentally, the best comment on this familiar slogan I ever heard was made by J. L. Austin. He said: "That's quite wrong; understanding might just add contempt to hatred."

morally praiseworthy or blameworthy *and* that no actions have hese properties. I want to say that the appearance of contradiction arises only if we assume the existence of some metaphysically absolute standpoint from which we can judge between the two standpoints I have been contrasting. But there is no such superior standpoint—or none that we know of; it is the idea of such a standpoint that is the illusion. Once that illusion is abandoned, the appearance of contradiction is dispelled. We can recognize, in our conception of the real, a reasonable relativity to standpoints that we do know and can occupy. Relative to the standpoint which we normally occupy as social beings, prone to moral and personal reactive attitudes, human actions, or some of them, are morally toned and propertied in the diverse ways signified in our rich vocabulary of moral appraisal. Relative to the detached naturalistic standpoint which we can sometimes occupy, they they have no properties but those which can be described in the vocabularies of naturalistic analysis and explanation (including, of course, psychological analysis and explanation).

It may seem that what I have just said is an evasion, rather than a solution, of a problem; that it is simply a refusal to face a real and difficult issue. Shortly I shall compare the case with that of another issue which, though on the face of it very different, is nevertheless, in an important respect, parallel to this one; so that they can be assessed together on this question of evasiveness.

But, first, I want to say something about the name and notion of *naturalism*. It will be apparent already that, as suggested in my introductory remarks, this notion has two faces; or at least two. I first invoked the notion, and the name, in connection with Hume and Hume's way with skepticism (including his own).

His point, echoed by Thomas Reid when he aligned himself with Hume the naturalist against Hume the skeptic, is that arguments, reasonings, either for or against the skeptical position, are, in practice, equally inefficacious and idle; since our natural disposition to belief, on the points challenged by the skeptic, is absolutely compelling and inescapable; neither shaken by skeptical argument nor reinforced by rational counter-argument. Where Nature thus determines us, we have an original non-rational commitment which sets the bounds within which, or the stage upon which, reason can effectively operate, and within which the question of the rationality or irrationality, justification or lack of justification, of this or that particular judgment or belief can come up. I then played roughly the same game, as one might put it, with the moral life. We are naturally social beings; and given with our natural commitment to social existence is a natural commitment to that whole web or structure of human personal and moral attitudes, feelings, and judgments of which I spoke. Our natural disposition to such attitudes and judgments is naturally secured against arguments suggesting that they are in principle unwarranted or unjustified just as our natural disposition to belief in the existence of body is naturally secured against arguments suggesting that it is in principle uncertain.

Thus far, our naturalist way with the moral skeptic parallels our naturalist way with the skeptic about the existence of the external world. But we have introduced, or acknowledged, a twist or complication in the moral case which has no parallel in the case of skepticism about the existence of body; and with this twist or complication the other face—or *another* face—of the notion of naturalism begins to show. For I acknowledged that we could theoretically, and sometimes can, and even sometimes must, practically, view human behavior, or stretches of human behavior, in a different light, which I characterized as "objective" or "detached" or (here comes the other face) "naturalistic"; a light which involves the partial or complete bracketing out or suspension of reactive feelings or moral attitudes or judgments. To see human beings and human actions in this light is to see them simply as objects and events in nature, natural objects and natural events, to be described, analyzed, and causally explained in terms in which moral evaluation has no place; in terms, roughly speaking, of an observational and theoretical vocabulary recognized in the natural and social sciences, including psychology. It was precisely the possibility of seeing human behavior in this naturalistic light, and the thought that this was exclusively the true light, that was held by the moral skeptic to undermine our sense of the appropriateness or general justification of those personal and moral reactive attitudes to which we are naturally prone.

So we see one species of naturalism set up in challenge to another. As I suggested in my introductory remarks, it will be useful to distinguish these two species of naturalism—or two faces of the notion of naturalism—by speaking of "reductive (or strict) naturalism" on the one hand and "nonreductive (or liberal or catholic) naturalism" on the other. It is reductive naturalism which holds that the naturalistic or objective view of human beings and human behavior undermines the validity of moral attitudes and reactions and displays moral judgment as no more than a vehicle of illusion. Nonreductive naturalism does not attempt to counter this alleged conclusion with argument, as some have done, alleging some non-natural, metaphysical foundation to validate our general disposition to moral response and moral judgment. (Cf. theories of noumenal freedom in Kant or of a special faculty of intuition of non-natural qualities in the ethical intuitionists of a recent generation.) The non-reductive naturalist simply urges, once again, the point that it is not open to us, it is simply not in our nature, to make a total surrender of those personal and moral reactive attitudes, those judgments of moral commendation or condemnation, which the reductive naturalist declares to be irrational as altogether lacking rational justification. The non-reductive naturalist's point is that there can only be a *lack* where there is a *need*. Questions of justification arise in plenty *within* the general framework of attitudes in question; but the existence of the general framework itself neither calls for nor permits an external reaction justification. (To put the point in Wittgenstein's idiom: This language-game, though its form may change with time or be subject to local variation, is one we cannot help playing; not one we choose.) It seems that the non-reductive naturalist might reasonably claim, if he cared to, to be the more thoroughgoing naturalist of the two. (He might even add pejorative stress to the last syllable of a description of his opponent as "merely naturalis*tic*.")

So much for the two faces of naturalism: the other complication in the case I have already mentioned. It is perfectly consistent with the adoption of the thoroughgoing or non-reductive naturalist's way with moral skepticism—his way with the reductive naturalist—to allow validity to the purely naturalistic view of human behavior. This can be done without prejudice to the general validity of moralistic views of the same thing, so long as we are prepared to acquiesce in the appropriate relativizations of our conception of the realities of the case. What from one point of view is rightly seen as a piece of disgraceful turpitude, an appropriate object of a reaction of moral disgust, is, from the other point of view, rightly seen as merely the natural outcome of a complex collocation of factors, an appropriate object of scientific, psychological, and sociological analysis and study.

3. A PARALLEL CASE: PERCEPTION AND ITS OBJECTS

I have remarked on the fact that many might find this relativizing move highly suspicious or evasive; and I promised to produce a parallel case.

The case I have in mind relates to the theory of sense-perception and of the nature of the material or physical things we see and feel, i.e. of the physical objects of sense-perception. It relates specifically to two contrasting views as to the nature of those objects, one of which might be called the view of unreflective or commonsense realism, the other the view of scientific realism. On the first view, the physical objects which we discriminate in ordinary speech and experience—tables, mountains, oranges, people and other animals—are, as A. J. Ayer happily expressed it, "visuo-tactile continuants."[6] That is to say, they really possess such phenomenal or sensible properties as we unreflectively credit them with: color-as-seen, i.e. color in the sense in which a painter or a child understands the term; visual shape; texture as felt. On the other view, the view of scientific realism, no such phenomenal properties really belong to physical objects at all. This view credits physical objects only with those properties which are mentioned in physical theory and physical explanation, including the causal explanation of our enjoyment of the kind of perceptual experience which we in fact enjoy and which is responsible for what is, on this view, the *illusion* that

6. Ayer, *The Central Questions of Philosophy* ch. 5 (London: Weidenfeld and Nicholson, 1973).

physical objects really are as we seem to perceive them as being. The scientific realist will typically lay considerable stress on the point that the character of our perceptual experience, the fact that we seem to perceive visuo-tactual objects in physical space, is causally accounted for by a combination of physical factors in describing which no mention is made of phenomenal properties; and that these factors include our own physical constitution, our physiological make-up. Had that make-up been radically different, we would not even have seemed to ourselves to perceive things in space as having the phenomenal properties we do seem to ourselves to perceive them as having. Had we been designed, say, as intelligent bats, we might instead have seemed to ourselves to perceive physical objects in space defined for us by a quite different range of phenomenal properties. But the real or intrinsic character of physical objects in space is clearly constant, whatever the variations in the physiological make-up of species that can be said to perceive them. So the phenomenal properties which, as it happens, *we* seem to ourselves to perceive as characterizing objects in space cannot properly be assigned to the objects as they really are. These phenomenal properties belong, at best, to the subjective character of our perceptual experience.

The commonsense realist, on the other hand, may lay stress on the depth and force of our habitual commitment to the view that, in favorable circumstances, we perceive things as they really are; that the sensible characteristics that we then seem to ourselves to perceive them as having really are theirs. (How else, indeed, could we attach aesthetic or sentimental value to things or persons?) And he may add the old point that we could not become perceptually aware of the primary qualities which scientific realism allows to physical things—of their shape, size, motion, and position—except by way of awareness of spatial boundaries defined in some sensory mode, e.g. by visual and tactile qualities such as scientific realism denies to the objects themselves. Now our very possession of the concept of physical space, hence the very possibility of research into the nature of its occupants, depends on such perceptual awareness of primary or spatial qualities of things. Hence the commonsense realist can plausibly argue that our natural prior commitment to the view of physical things as sensibly or phenomenally propertied is a necessary precondition of our even entertaining the view of scientific realism which would deny them such properties; and if he is polemically minded enough and senses an irreconcilable antagonism between the two views, he may be disposed to descend to the abusive language of polemics and dismiss the scientific view as no form of realism at all, as a misguided attempt to displace the rich reality of the world in favor of a bloodless abstraction—or something of the kind; which would no doubt provoke his opponent to charge him with infantile attachment to primitive modes of thought, immature incapacity to face impersonal realities, and so forth.

All such rhetorical extravagance is out of place, however; and the impression of irreconcilable antagonism between the two views disappears as soon as we are prepared to recognize, as before, a certain ultimate relativity in our conception of the real; in this case, of the real properties of physical objects. Relative to the human perceptual standpoint, commonplace physical objects really are what Ayer calls visuo-tactile continuants, bearers of phenomenal visual and tactile properties. Relative to the standpoint of physical science (which is also a human standpoint) they really have no properties but those recognized, or to be recognized, in physical theory, and are really constituted in ways which can only be described in what, from the phenomenal point of view, are abstract terms. Once the relativity of these "really"s to different standpoints, to different standards of "the real" is acknowledged, the appearance of contradiction between these positions disappears; the same thing can both be, and not be, phenomenally propertied.

4. EVASION OR SOLUTION? RECONCILIATION OR SURRENDER?

The parallel between my two examples of a relativizing, reconciling move is obvious enough. And to a hard-line adherent of the position which he himself will describe as objective or scientific both solutions will appear to have parallel weaknesses. Both will appear as substantial surrenders to his own position which have been disguised as agreements in order to conceal or shy away from what is felt to be the unpalatable truth. Let us look further into this.

It is worth remarking, first, that in both cases there are features which, on the one hand, may seem to make the relativity thesis easier to accept and yet, on the other, may seem simply to display its weakness and underline the force of the hard-liner's insistence that the view he rejects really does rest on illusion, and that his own view really is a *correction* of the rejected view. The point I have in mind is easily illustrated for the perceptual case. It is the point that relativity of the concept of "real property" to shifting standards of "the real" may manifest itself *within* one of the two standpoints I distinguished, viz. the human perceptual standpoint. We are generally disposed to take normal sighting or handling conditions as setting the standard for the real color or shape or texture of an object. But we may sometimes be induced to shift our standard and adopt that set by the appearance of the object under microscopic examination. Any suggestion of contradiction in *this* case is readily and easily resolved by recognizing the relativity of our phenomenal-property ascriptions to these shifting standards. Thus (to repeat an example I have used elsewhere[7]) we are quite content to say, and can without contradiction say, both that blood is really uniformly bright red and also that it is really mostly colorless. Since we can thus shift our point of view within the general framework of human perception, it is suggested that we should see the shift to the viewpoint of scientific realism as simply a more radical shift to a point *outside* that framework, but no more to be thought of as generating irreconcilable conflict than shifts *within* it.

Evidently there is no exact parallel between the cases of phenomenal properties of physical objects and moral properties of human behavior or between varying preceptual viewpoints taken as standard and varying moral viewpoints taken as standard. Where moral standards are concerned, we are not so lightheartedly ready to shift from one to another and back again. But though there are dissimilarities, there are also similarities. We can at least understand the possibility of moral viewpoints other than our own. One might say that it is part of being an educated person to be able to understand such viewpoints in a fuller sense, i.e. to have an imaginative grasp of what it would be, or was, or is, like to hold them. This is the easier for us to the extent that we are prepared to welcome a certain degree of moral pluralism, a certain diversity of moral outlook; and we may be the readier to do this because, since it is easy to form an exaggerated

7. Strawson, "Perception and Its Objects," in C. F. Macdonald, ed., *Perception and Identity* (London: Macmillan, 1979).

impression of the consistency of our own and others' moral outlook, many of us, as a result of causes partly historical and partly
idiosyncratic, contain different moralities within ourselves; even
though one reasonably consistent set of standards may be dom-
inant in most of us. As for the magnitude of *historical* shifts in
standards, that is a commonplace: consider the changes in the
attitude to the institution of slavery, now generally regarded as
morally abhorrent; consider even possible future changes in the
attitude to meat-eating, which some wish to see generally regarded as no less morally abhorrent.

To draw attention thus to the diversity of moral viewpoints is
not to deny the existence of what is universal or unifying in them.
Certain relatively vaguely or abstractly conceived characteristics—such as generosity, justice, honesty—are generally recognized as morally admirable (as virtues) and their opposites as
morally deplorable, even though the specific forms in which they
are recognized may vary. And, perhaps more to the point, there
is a general willingness to concede some measure of moral ap-
probation to anyone who acts rightly "by his own lights," as we
say, whatever they may be; to anyone who "obeys his con-
science" or "acts as it seems to him that he ought to act" or
"does his duty as he sees it," and so on. This still leaves us a
long way from an exact parallel with the perceptual case. We
are not as willing to accord equal validity to, say, the Homeric
and the liberal bourgeois visions of the good, of morally admirable behavior, as we are to accord equal validity to the microscopic and the normal-sighted visions of material surfaces. We
are not as willing to say that moral truth is relative to moral
standard as we are to say that truth about phenomenal properties, color, or texture, is relative to choice of visual-perceptual
medium. But still the recognition of diversity of moral stand-

points and the possibility of sympathy with different standpoints introduces us to the idea of sympathy with different moral judgements or reactive assessments which are incompatible with one another if unrelativized to their appropriate standards but between which the incompatibility disappears if the relativization is made explicit. And this, it is suggested, makes it easier to see how there disappears also the apparently more radical opposition between the view, common to all these standpoints, that there is a moral reality for such judgments more or less adequately to represent and the view, from the detached or "objective" or "naturalistic" standpoint, that there is no such reality— once, that is, the appropriate relativization is made.

So much, then, by way of exposition of the thesis that recognition of these relativities internal to the human perceptual and moralistic standpoints makes it easier to accept the more radical relativizing move in each case; the move which, in the one case, seeks to reconcile the ascription of phenomenal, visuo-tactile properties to physical things with the denial that they have any such properties; and which, in the other case, seeks to reconcile the view that human actions are proper objects of moral praise or blame and personal and moral reactive attitudes in general with the view what such attitudes lack all validity and appropriateness, have no objective basis or justification.

I remarked, however, when I introduced the point, that this acknowledgment of internal relativities has a double-edged character. It might be exploited in the reconciling way I have just indicated. But it also lends itself to exploitation by the scientistic hard-liners in a quite opposed sense. They might argue as follows. These internal relativities simply underline the wholly subjective character of these alleged phenomenal or moral characteristics of things or actions. Pointing them out is simply pointing out that one and the same thing, without its real or intrinsic character varying at all, may causally produce quite different subjective experiences or reactions in variant circumstances and in different subjects. There can be no objective truth of the matter where there are so many competing candidates for the position, each claiming its own validity, and no impartial or external criterion for judging between them. How different the position is with the objective or scientific standpoint. Of course it is not denied that scientific theory, physical theory, concerning the real constitution of physical bodies changes or develops over time. Nor is it denied that, even though the common repertoire of concepts for the recording or description of human behavior remains relatively constant over time, the theories of causal explanation of such behavior also show change and development, especially in recent times—with notable repercussions on the descriptive repertoire. But what we have here is not simple diversity of view, but cumulative advance or development in knowledge. Here there are precisely what is lacking in the other cases, namely objective tests and standards for evaluating theories: notably the test of verification, the harsh test of success or failure in prediction and control.

Moreover, the hard-liners might go on, the objective or scientific view of the real can absorb or assimilate into itself all the actual phenomena out of which the rival views weave their illusions of reality. For these actual phenomena are simply subjective experiences and reactions of which the scientific approach can indeed acknowledge the reality *as such* (i.e. as subjective experiences and reactions) and of which it is ready and equipped to offer a causal analysis, a causal account.

To this the patient reply must be: not that it is mistaken to think of the physical world in the abstract terms of physical science which allow no place in it for phenomenal qualities; nor that it is mistaken to think of the world of human behavior in the purely naturalistic terms which exclude moral praise or blame; only that it is mistaken to think of these views of the world as genuinely incompatible with the view of physical things as being, in the most unsophisticated sense of these words, colored or plain, hard or soft, noisy or silent; and with the view of human actions as, sometimes, noble or mean, admirable or despicable, good or evil, right or wrong. Though we can, by an intellectual effort, occupy at times, and for a time, the former pair of standpoints, we cannot give up the latter pair of standpoints. This last is the point on which the non-reductive naturalist, as I have called him, insists. What the relativizing move does is to remove the appearance of incompatibility between members of the two pairs of views. Without the relativizing move, the scientific hard-liner, or reductive naturalist, could stick to his line; admitting that we are naturally committed to the human perceptual and morally reactive viewpoints, he could simply conclude that we live most of our lives in a state of unavoidable illusion. The relativizing move averts this (to most) unpalatable conclusion. It would surely be an extreme of self-mortifying intellectual Puritanism which would see in this very fact a reason for rejecting that move.

3.

The Mental and
the Physical

1. THE POSITION SO FAR

I have invoked what I have called Naturalism in two very different kinds of connection. First, I invoked it as supplying a way of dealing with certain kinds of traditional skepticism; and as a better, because more realistic, way than any attempt to justify or validate by rational argument those very general beliefs which traditional skepticism seeks to put in doubt or to represent as uncertain. The point was that our commitment on these points is pre-rational, natural, and quite inescapable, and sets, as it were, the natural limits within which, and only within which, the serious operations of reason, whether by way of questioning or of justifying beliefs, can take place. ("Serious" = "actually making a difference.") There was no question here of a relativizing move, for there was no question of an alternative view of the way things really are, associated with an alternative standpoint which can be seriously occupied.

Second, I invoked Naturalism in connection with our equally deep-rooted disposition to regard ordinary bodies, i.e., common physical objects, as phenomenally propertied and to regard human agents and their actions as proper objects of moral attitudes, i.e. as bearers of moral or ethical attributes. But here the situation is different. For though I think it is true that it is no more possible to reason us out of these dispositions than it is to reason us into serious doubt about the existence of physical objects or other people, yet we are, in the case of these dispositions, provided with a standpoint or standpoints which we can seriously occupy and from which we can form a different conception of the real nature of the objects of these dispositions, a conception which leaves no room for phenomenal properties or moral attributes of those objects. And here we see that inherent in the possibility of occupying these alternative standpoints is the temptation to claim exclusive correctness for them, to claim that they alone yield the correct conception of the real nature of things; that the only reality represented by our ascriptions to objects, agents, or actions of phenomenal or moral attributes is the possession by those objects, agents, or actions of non-phenomenal or non-moral properties which invoke in us certain experiences or responses. This is what I called reductive naturalism. It presents us with a conception of the world as, so to speak, morally and literally colorless. The operation is, of course, a two-stage one: the stripping of the world of moral qualities leaves it perceptible; the stripping of it of phenomenal qualities leaves it imperceptible as it really is. I have wanted to say, not that these conceptions of the world are wrong, but that the world, as conceived from these standpoints, is not the world as experienced; it is not, as one might say in Paris, *le monde vécu*. Hence the relativizing move. We lack reason for saying either that the scientific-objective standpoint or that the human-perceptual-and-moral standpoint gives us the exclusively correct type of conception of the real nature of things. We could have such a reason only if there were a standpoint we could occupy which was superior to either. But there is no such standpoint.

2. THE IDENTITY THESIS: THE TWO STORIES
AND THEIR INTERFACE

I turn now to an issue which might initially seem to promise, if not a perfect parallel, at least some similarity to the two last; and we shall see, in the end, that there is indeed a certain similarity, a partial parallel, though it is not located just where it might at first seem to be.

What I have in mind is a certain doctrine which is currently popular, at least as a topic of discussion. It is the doctrine, known as the identity thesis, that events or states belonging to a person's mental history—his feelings, thoughts, sensations, perceptual experiences, emotional states, standing beliefs and so on—are, all of them, identical with events or states belonging to his physical history, his history as a physical organism; in brief, that mental events and states are a subclass of physical events and states, of the kind that form the subject-matter of neurophysiology. This thesis is affirmed by some philosophers and denied by others; and it might appear as if we have here a straightforward conflict between a reductive materialism on the one hand and a more or less outraged affirmation of the existence of consciousness on the other. But the situation is not so simple.

It would, of course, seem precisely as simple as that to anyone who subscribed to a two-substance or Cartesian view of persons; who held that a person consisted of a peculiarly intimate union of two distinct individual substances, a mind and a body, each the subject of its own distinct kinds of state and changes of state. To him the identity thesis would appear patently false, since no event happening to an individual of one of these kinds (a mind), or state of such an individual, could even be of the same kind as, let alone identical with, an event happening to, or state of, a distinct individual of the other kind (a body). But this simple dismissal is evidently not available to one who rejects the two-substance view, as I think many, perhaps most, now do, in favor of the concept of a person as a concept of a type of unitary being irreducibly and essentially, though not exhaustively, characterizable as one which satisfies both psychological, or mentalistic, and material, or physicalistic, predicates. (I say, not exhaustively, since some non-human animals which fall short of satisfying the requirements for personhood may be held to answer to this characterization as it stands; but it will serve for our purposes.) For, given this unitary concept, given that what is irreducibly one and the same individual may simultaneously satisfy both mental and physical predicates, may it not indeed also be the case that one and the same particular *state* of such an individual may have both a physical and a mental aspect (or description); and that one and the same change of state of such an individual, i.e. one and the same *event* happening to that individual, may have both a physical and a mental aspect (or description)? The thesis we are to consider, expressed in these terms, is not, of course, that every such state or change of state which has a physical description also has a mental description, but the converse, i.e. that every state or change of state which has a mental description has also a physical description: hence the summary formula, "mental events are a subclass of physical events."

As anyone who has familiarized himself with the literature on this topic will know, a great deal of complicated and more or less subtle argument has been devoted to the issue, much of it turning on the notion of causation. My intention, however, is not to join in the argument directly, but, rather, as far as possible, to circumvent it. First, let me remark on a trivial truth. In so far as we are prepared to recognize something which we might call "the total state of a person at a given moment," it will be true that we are countenancing something which certainly admits of at least a physical and, for a great part of the time, both a physical and a mental description. But this concession will be quite inadequate to satisfy the adherents of the identity theory; for this concession would be formally consistent with such a total state having distinct particular components, some mental, some physical, with none of the former being identical with any of the latter; whereas the adherents of the identity theory are contending for the existence of identities between the mental and the physical in the case of *each* mental item forming part of the total state; though they are not in general interested in specifying these identities nor indeed think it in general possible to specify them. For instance, they would maintain that such an event as a man's suddenly noticing the date is strictly identical with some event (e.g. some firing of neurons) describable in neurophysiological terms; and that his ensuing state of believing, say, that it is his wife's birthday is identical with some physical condition describable in such terms.

Setting aside the refinements of current argument, let us try to come at the most general considerations which underlie the debate. First, it seems increasingly reasonable, or at least not unreasonable, to make a certain assumption: viz. that there is a system of physical law such that all bodily movements of human beings, including, of course, those that are involved in speech, are the causal outcome of the stimulation of sensory surfaces together with the internal physical constitution of the organism, those movements being causally mediated by electro-chemical events within the organism, and the constitution of the latter being itself constantly modified by events in its own history. Seen from this limited point of view, the whole history of a human being could in principle, though not in practice, be told in these terms. So told, of course, the history would leave out almost everything that was humanly interesting, either to the subject of it or to anyone else. We have another and more familiar style of talking about ourselves and others, in which we speak of action and behavior (in the ordinary sense of this latter word), rather than simply of limbs moving, and in which we freely use the language of sensations, perceptions, thoughts, memories, assertions, beliefs, desires, and intentions; in short, mentalistic or personalistic language. In practice, of course, we are never able to tell the complete history of a person in these terms either, not even when that person is oneself. Still, we have the theoretical idea of the two histories, each complete in its own terms; we might call them the physical history and the personal history, admitting, of course, that the latter, the personal history, will include accounts of physical action, reaction and displacement as well as mental events and states Each story will invoke its own explanatory connections, the one in terms of neurophysiological and anatomical laws, the other in terms of what is sometimes called, with apparently pejorative intent, "folk psychology"; i.e., the ordinary explanatory terms employed by diarists, novelists, biographers, historians, journalists, and gossips, when they deliver their accounts of human behavior and human experience—the terms employed by such simple folk as Shakespeare, Tolstoy, Proust, and Henry James.

No one supposes that there is any practical possibility of a complete mapping of a personal story on to the corresponding physical story: i.e. of correlating each ascription to a person of a state or event belonging to his personal history with a corresponding ascription to that person of a state or event belonging to his physical history. (There is nothing question-begging about my use of "correlation" here; even if it were held that the items ascribed in the correlated ascriptions were identical, the ascriptions are clearly not identical.) But equally no one supposes that the two stories are quite independent of each other or, more precisely, that the facts reported in the personal story are unrelated to the facts reported in the physical story. Indeed a great part of the interest in neurophysiological investigations depends precisely on the existence of an intimate relation between *types* of fact which belong to the personal story and *types* of fact which belong to the physical story: such investigations are properly described as investigations into, e.g., the physical basis of memory, the physiology of pain, the nature of thirst, etc. The results achieved, and promised, by these investigations make it reasonable to draw a conclusion which is commonly drawn and which can be expressed without using the controversial concept of identity and without prejudice either way on the controversial issue: the conclusion, namely, that each *particular* mental event or state belonging to a personal history has a *particular* physical basis or is *physically realized* (as the phrase goes) in a *particular* physical event or state belonging to the corresponding physical history; even though the description of the particular physical realization of a particular mental event or state would no doubt be very complicated, if it could be given at all, and even though there is, as remarked, no practical possibility of an exhaustive mapping of particular mental event- or state-ascriptions on to such particular physical realization or physical basis ascriptions.

3. IDENTITY OR CAUSAL LINKAGE?

All the preceding may seem like unhelpful skirmishing on the outskirts of the real question. The real question, it may be said, is this: what is the relation between the particular mental event or state and its physical basis or realization? Is it that of strict identity, so that we have in each case just one item, though susceptible, in principle, of two quite luridly distinct descriptions, one couched in purely physical (physiological) terms, the other couched in mentalistic or experiential terms? Or is it a relation of causal linkage between two distinct items, one, say, a physical event, the other, say, an experience? Should a sequence of relevant occurrences in a segment of the life history of a person be represented as in figure 1? or as in figure 2?

FIGURE 1

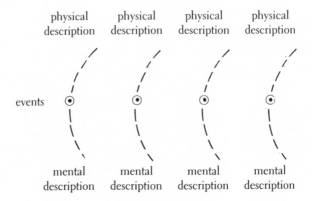

| physical description | physical description | physical description | physical description |

events

| mental description | mental description | mental description | mental description |

FIGURE 2

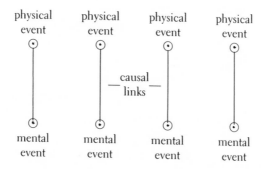

It might even be suggested that we could have a third diagram which allows for only one particular item in each case (and to that extent agrees with figure 1), but provides that item with two distinct kinds of property or quality, the two distinct qualities or properties being causally related thus:

FIGURE 3

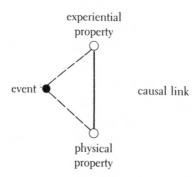

But figure 3 must either allow the *occurrence* of the experiential-property-*instance* and the *occurrence* of the physical-property-*in-*

stance as distinct events, in which case (since events are not substances) it collapses into figure 2, or insist that they too are the same, in which case it collapses into figure 1.

Perhaps we should consider, however, whether all pictures of this kind are not misleadingly crude. What *are* the events we are concerned with? They are events happening to, or in, people. (This is not something extrinsic to their nature.) Take a particular subject, a person, John. Suppose John suddenly recognizes an old friend in the crowd: he suddenly sees a face *as* the face of his old friend. In describing the event, we are predicating something—an instantaneous property, one might say—*of John.* Can we localize the event, determine where it happened? Yes, for we can determine where John was when it happened. It happened to John, say, in Victoria Station under the clock. What about the event's phyical basis or physical realization? Well, perhaps it consisted in the occurrence of such-and-such a brainevent in the context of a particular organization of the brain and nervous system in general. This can be localized too, but, it seems, in a narrower or more exact fashion, inside John's skin, in or throughout a particular region of his brain and nervous system. There is no decisive argument from difference of location here, however, since we can also determine that the physical realization-event happened to or in John in Victoria Station under the clock; and we might think it mere prejudice or habit or lack of information that inhibits our stating that John's recognition of his friend was located in or throughout a particular region of his brain and nervous system.

However, it is not mere prejudice. Rather, it is implicit acknowledgment of the fact (which at least one exponent of a version of the identity theory is ready enough to acknowledge explicitly[1]) that the two different accounts (for the accounts are certainly different) of what happened to or in John at that moment in Victoria Station belong to two different stories about John, stories told from two different points of view. One is the point of view of the diarist or biographer, recounting the history of John as a person. The other is the point of view of a physical scientist, recounting the history of John viewed as an electro-chemical-physical organism. We may suppose, contrary to fact, that the second story could be complete: mentioning all stimulation to sensory surfaces, giving a full account of internal structure and the history of its modifications, tracing the complete causal paths from stimulation to movement of limbs, tongue, head, and organs. Nothing, we suppose, would be left out; and there would be no causal or explanatory gap anywhere. We may suppose an equally coherent and full account to be given in the personal terms of the biogapher's story. Again no mysteries are left.

Our problem arises because we have supposed, and shall continue to suppose, a certain kind of interface between the two stories, which we expressed by saying that every mental state or mental happening attributed to John in the personal history has a physical basis or realization describable in the terms of the physical story. We will preserve that supposition. But what I am going to suggest is that instead of pressing the choice between the two pictures I mentioned earlier, we should leave the matter where it is, i.e. be content with the admittedly noncommittal formula which speaks of a physical realization of the mental. To do otherwise is to fail to acknowledge the extent to which the

1. Donald Davidson, *Actions and Events* (London: Oxford, 1980), *passim*.

two stories are not *in pari materia*. It is to attempt a unified story where none is to be had.

One can see, easily enough, a sense in which *an* identity-claim can be admitted; but only because, in this sense, it is metaphysically innocuous. Thus one can say: *from the exclusively physicobiological point of view*, what, in the other story, is called John's recognition of his friend simply *is* the relevant particular brain-event occurring in the context of a particular organization of his nervous system. What makes this remark metaphysically innocuous or noncommittal is the governing rubric, "from the exclusively physicobiological point of view." From that point of view, indeed, what we are *really* referring to, in our ascription to John of the experience of recognition, is the relevant physical event; but, again, the "really" here gets all its force from the governing rubric. So the apparent identity is obtained simply by bracketing out the personal story in favor of the physical story. We have made no step, such as a genuine identity theory would require, toward unifying the stories.

I would go further and enunciate the general point that we have no genuine practical *use* for the concept of identity here; and where we have no genuine practical use for it, we have no metaphysical use either.

Should we then settle for the alternative picture of causal correlation between physical realization and experiental event? Of the two pictures in question this may seem, by contrast, the more acceptable. But there are difficulties. One objection commonly brought against it is that it reduces mental events to the status of epiphenomena, "nomological danglers," caused events with no causal efficacy—since, on the assumption with which we are working, it would be in principle be possible to trace an uninterrupted causal route through the physical organism from sensory-surface stimulation to gross bodily movement without reference to mental intermediaries; whereas this epiphenomenalist consequence is avoided by the identity thesis. This objection is unsound. But the reason why it is unsound is also a reason for viewing the causal picture with rather little favor or enthusiasm.

The objection is unsound because no one can suppose that tracing the physical causal route through the physical organism (assuming, what is false, that it could in practice be done) would in fact yield a causal explanation of human *action*, of human *behavior*. Any explanatory account of a person's behavior (a much misused word) belongs firmly to the personal story, the biographer's or diarist's story, and mentions, as causally explanatory factors, just those mental events and states (desires, perceptions, beliefs, decisions) which the objection represents as epiphenomenal, as lacking causal efficacy, and which would indeed have to be so regarded if we thought that the only coherent explanatory story was the physical one.

But though this is a good reason for rejecting the objection as unsound, it is also, as I suggested, the reason why we cannot view with much complacency or great satisfaction the causal picture of the relation between experiential event and physical realization. The notion of "cause" has a *use* for us when we can associate it with understanding and explanation or, more practically, and derivatively, with prediction and/or control. But even if we could establish (which, in general, we cannot) the *specific detail* of a particular physical realization of a particular mental event or state, the fact would generally have no part to play in the explanatory account of the behavior of the person to whose history that particular mental event or state belonged. That account, to repeat what has just been said, belongs firmly to the personal story, the biographer's or diarist's story, which, as Davidson, for one, is often concerned to stress,[2] is answerable to a set of constraints quite discrepant from those which govern the (in any case hypothetical) other story, the complete causal story of the purely physical organism.

If, however, we feel the need to "keep our metaphysics warm" by plumping for either the identity picture or the causal picture, then we should probably plump, though without much enthusiasm, for the latter. I say, without much enthusiasm; but I do not mean, without any. For we shall certainly learn more and more about the *general* causal dependence of the conscious enjoyment or exercise of our various experiential capacities (e.g. for vision, memory, recognition) on physical mechanisms, even though we are not likely to establish, and there would be little interest in establishing, extended point-to-point correspondences between particular (token) experiences, as fully described in the idiom of personal histories, and physiological (token) events, as fully described in the idiom of physical histories.

4. AN IMPERFECT PARALLEL

The reader may have wondered why I, even tentatively, suggested a parallel between the question we have just been considering and the two discussed earlier, regarding morality and sense-perception respectively. The differences certainly seem considerable. In the earlier two cases we had the appearance of a radical conflict of a distinctive kind: a conflict between objective or naturalistic or scientific views of the world, according to which a certain range of attitudes to human behavior and a certain set of common beliefs about physical things embodied or

2. *Ibid.*

rested on illusion, and, on the other side, a common commitment to those very attitudes and beliefs, a view of the world according to which those attitudes and beliefs corresponded in general, though not necessarily in particular, to moral and sensible reality. And the conflict was to be resolved by what I called the relativizing move: relativizing the concept of reality to distinct, even opposed, but not strictly incompatible, standpoints or points of view. On the face of it, the present case offers no obvious parallel to this. The conflict appears, rather, to be over the relation between aspects of reality—the physiological and the experiential—with neither side declaring either aspect to be illusory or to fall short of full reality. So there is no question of resolving *this* conflict by acknowledging two different standpoints from one of which one aspect exhausts the reality, while from the other of which this is not so. This does not seem to be how the case stands at all.

However, let us look again. First, notice that it might be said that if we *are* to find a parallel with our earlier issues, it is not by trying to reconcile the two conflicting sides that we shall succeed in doing so, not by trying to resolve the conflict, but by embracing one of the conflicting views, namely the identity thesis. In an earlier case, we wanted to say that one and the same thing, a physical object, is, from the human perceptual standpoint, the bearer of phenomenal sensible qualities and yet is, from the standpoint of physical science, the bearer of no properties but those recognized in physical theory. Is not this reminiscent of the identity thesis itself? For, according to it, *one and the same event* which, from the personal or biographical standpoint, may be correctly described as the subject's undergoing some conscious experience or being the subject of some mental event, yet is, from the physiological standpoint, correctly and fully described as the subject's undergoing some physiological change of state.

Well, in a way, one might be tempted to accept that. But— and here I must repeat what I have said already—what one might find acceptable in that surely falls short of what was intended by the adherents of the identity thesis. For what one finds acceptable is no more than the truth that, speaking physiologically, what happens to the subject when he undergoes some conscious experience is just some physiological event; and this truth is a truism perfectly compatible with the doctrine that the subject's undergoing the conscious experience is something over and above the occurrence in him of the physiological event, even though inseparably connected with it; hence a truism perfectly compatible with the doctrine that appeared as a rival to the identity thesis. What gave the impression of a yielding to, or acceptance of, the identity thesis was the occurrence of the phrase "one and the same event." What may dispel that impression, preserving what legitimately underlies the identity thesis, while discarding the dubious operation with the notion of identity, is the substitution of the phrase "what happens to the subject." We may indeed say that what happens to the subject is, from the subjective or biographical point of view, his undergoing the conscious experience and, from the physical scientist's or physiological point of view, the occurrence in him of the physiological event; but here the appearance of operating with the notion of identity disappears altogether (except as regards the subject himself); for there is no reason to construe the phrase "what happens to the subject" as referring to a single event-item. Where we may indeed operate freely with the notion of identity is with respect to the subject himself, a being both conscious and corporeal, one and the same subject of both the personal and the physiological histories.

I have spoken of what legitimately underlies, without legitimating, the identity thesis. I refer to the reasonable assumption that we are, at least, physical systems the physical movements (not "behavior") of which are the causal outcome of their physical stimulations and physical constitution, and every "mental movement" of which (if I may use the expression) has a physical basis or realization. We can accept this as a working assumption, while rejecting the crudely dualistic, or two-substance, picture of a kind of inner causal tennis-match between mind and body, a picture which still has its adherents. Rejecting this picture does not, of course, involve rejecting the explanatory personal history as we in fact tell it.

I doubt, however, whether these legitimate and reasonable considerations are all that, in all cases, underlie the identity thesis. They are hardly sufficient to explain the form it takes or the passionate intensity with which some of its adherents hold to it. And I suspect that what less legitimately, or at any rate less sympathetically, underlies the thesis is, in some cases, a kind of reductive naturalism which might reasonably be called "scientism": a dismissive attitude to whatever cannot be exhaustively described and accounted for in the terms of physical science; an attitude which, in its extreme form, amounts, in the present context, to a refusal to recognize the existence of subjective or conscious experience altogether. J. L. Mackie, in his book on Locke,[3] suggests that both Smart and Armstrong are in effect committed to such a refusal; and Mackie, having in general strong sympathies with the scientific attitude, is by no means a hostile witness here.

Perhaps it will now be clearer why I spoke of a parallel with issues discussed earlier. For there is an evident affinity, though

3. Mackie, *Problems from Locke* (London: Oxford, 1976), ch. 5, p. 169.

by no means identity, between the scientism that pooh-poohs subjective experience, and scientific realism which relegates phenomenal qualities to the realm of the subjective, denying them objective reality, and the reductive naturalism that represents moral and personal reactive attitudes as resting on illusion, denying, in effect, the objective reality of moral desert, or moral good and evil. All these stances have in common, though in different degrees, a reductive and scientistic tendency which leads me to bring them together under the label of "reductive naturalism." It would be stretching the word a little, but not perhaps too much, to represent them also as varieties of *skepticism:* moral skepticism, skepticism about the world as it appears, skepticism about the mental. Skepticism is not really the *mot juste*—reductivism is better—so I do not want to lay stress on it. I want simply to say that against all these reductivist (or skeptical) stances, as also against skepticism more traditionally and properly so-called, I have tried to set up another kind of Naturalism—a non-reductive variety—which recognizes the human inescapability and metaphysical acceptability of those various types of conception of reality which are challenged or put in doubt by reductive or traditionally skeptical arguments.

We shall see the parallel extend yet further and into less obvious regions of philosophical debate.

4.

The Matter of Meaning

1. INTENSIONAL ENTITIES: REJECTIONISTS AND THEIR OBLIGATIONS

The particular region I have in mind might be called, not altogether satisfactorily, that of the theory of meaning; or, perhaps better, the matter of meaning. We all talk, ordinarily and readily enough, of the *senses* of words; of the *meanings* of words and sentences; and of the *concepts* which words (or some words) express. We also talk of *attributes, properties, kinds,* and *types;* and philosophers, at least, sometimes speak collectively of all these as *universals,* contrasting them thereby with their *particular* exemplifications or instances or tokens.

Again, we talk ordinarily and readily enough of, e.g., *What John said;* of *its* being believed or doubted by Peter; of Paul denying *it;* of William saying *the same thing,* though in different words; of *its* being more elegantly expressed in French by Yvette; of *its* being true (or false); and so on. On the face of it, the nounphrases and attendant pronouns here do not refer to the token words, the token sentence, which John uttered; or, indeed, to the type-sentence of which he uttered a token; or even to the meaning of that sentence, since the same type-sentence, with constant and unambiguous meaning, can be used to say different things with different truth-values (as is the case with any sentence containing deictic or indexical elements). Once again, the philosophers have a word for it—or several words: they may speak, with Frege, of the *thought* expressed by the utterance; or of the *proposition* or *propositional content* asserted, denied, believed, surmised, true or false; or even of the *statement* made, doubted, denied, reaffirmed in different words, true or false.

In general, it is true of both these groups of nouns, noun-phrases and attendant pronouns that the things they appear to stand for or refer to—if there are such things—are abstract objects, not natural objects. They are not found in nature. They are not locatable in space or datable in time. A particular utterance or inscription of a proposition is a natural occurrence or object, an auditory phenomenon or a physical mark, but the proposition expressed is not. Someone's thinking of a sense or meaning and someone's recognizing something as an instance of, or as exemplifying, a universal, a kind or property, are again natural occurrences, mental events that occur in nature. But the sense or meaning, the property or universal themselves are not natural objects. If they are objects at all, they are objects of thought alone, not objects encounterable in nature or occurring in the natural world. Again, what a proposition is about is often a particular natural thing, what falls under a concept or exemplifies or instantiates a universal is generally a particular thing or occurrence in nature; but these relations of "falling under," "exemplifying," "instantiating," or "being about" are not relations themselves exemplified in nature, i.e. not relations between one natural thing and another. The non-natural abstract entities I speak of—if indeed there are such things—are sometimes called "intensions" or "intensional entities."

Naturally (I stress the word), the notion that there are indeed such things as these abstract or intensional entities, objects of thought but not natural objects, gives rise to suspicion and even hostility. It will especially do so among those predisposed toward reductive naturalism. But even among those of a more liberal or catholic outlook there is a strong natural inclination to believe that whatever exists at all exists in nature, that the domain of the existent is coexistent with the domain of objects and occurrences in space and time. So there is no room for abstract entities; not because admitting them would result in overcrowding (though people do indeed sometimes speak in these terms, of, e.g., an "overpopulated" universe), but for precisely the opposite reason: they do not even compete for spaces and dates, any more than fictitious characters do. Indeed—there is a strong inclination to say—they are fictions themselves. Apart from this natural inclination to deny that there are such things as universals, concepts, propositions etc., on the ground that all that exists are natural objects and occurrences, another charge sometimes leveled against them is that belief in such entities commits the believer to what has been called a "pernicious mentalism." We shall see the point of this charge later.

Now of course any philosopher disposed to reject intensional entities as pseudo-entities, for the reasons indicated or for others, is nevertheless bound to acknowledge that the various nominal expressions which appear to stand for such entities (if they stand for anything) have a large currency in our language; that indeed they appear often to be used to say things that are true. (I mean quite ordinary commonplace things such as that someone knows the *meaning* of a certain expression; or that two expressions have the *same meaning* or differ in meaning; or that someone has grasped, or failed to grasp, the *sense* of a certain sentence; or that someone has mastered a certain *concept*; or we may inquire into the etymology of a word, where what we are inquiring about seems to be, not the particular token we utter, but the *type* of which it is a token; or we may say that something is a good example of a certain *property* or is distinguished by the possession of a certain *attribute*.) Clearly, then, the rejectionist philosopher is under an obligation to give some account of these and other ordinary uses of the expressions in question in terms which he regards as acceptable, i.e. in terms which do not carry even an apparent commitment to theoretical recognition of the entities he rejects.

The obligation extends beyond such simple examples as I have given. There is, or was, a traditional distinction, i.e. a distinction well established in the philosophical tradition, between "truths of reason," as Leibniz called them, and truths of fact; or between necessary and contingent truths, where the notion of necessity is not to be understood as natural or physical necessity, not a matter of natural law, but rather as what is variously characterized as "logical" or "semantic" or "analytic" or "conceptual" necessity. (I do not mean to suggest that these expressions have always been used synonymously, or with the same intended extension, in this context; but they have, in this context, been generally used to carry an implied contrast with natural necessity.) Attempts to elucidate this notion, or these notions, of necessary truth have rested heavily on the notion of meaning. Such truths or propositions, if there are such, cannot be thought of as expressing facts about the natural world, since they are supposed to hold true whatever may be the case in nature. They are supposed to hold true quite independently of the natural facts. So they are sometimes supposed to express relations between the *meanings* of the expressions which occur in their formulations; or to express relations between the universal or other abstract entities, such as numbers, signified by some of those expressions. If they are truths about anything at all, if they say anything, it seems that they must be truths about such objects of thought alone, concepts, universals, abstract entities. Since they are held to be consistent with any state of affairs whatever in the natural world, they say nothing about—convey no information or misinformation about—that world. And here we see the source of the appeal, for those who think that every genuine truth must be a truth about the natural world, of the striking remark that all of what are called necessary truths say the same thing, namely nothing.

We can put aside this striking remark since, in its own epigrammatic, if slightly perverse, way, it is an endorsement, rather than a rejection, of the existence of this distinct class of propositions. (Even if those who make it jib at speaking of truth here, they implicitly recognize that the validity or acceptability of such seeming propositions is independent of natural facts, of how things are in the natural world.) What we have to consider, rather, is the position of the thoroughgoing anti-intensionalist, the determined reductive naturalist, who must question the existence of any genuine, ultimate, irreducible distinction of this kind; as Quine, for example, has most famously done.[1] And this is where the rejectionist's further obligation arises. For the tradition sufficiently shows that there do exist intuitions of conceptual or logical necessity, even if such intuitions are illusory; that people do suppose that they grasp or perceive necessary relations between abstract objects or concepts, even if there are no such

1. N. V. Quine, "Two Dogmas of Empiricism," in *From a Logical Point of View* (Cambridge: Harvard University Press, 1953), and elsewhere.

perceptions, no such relations, no such objects to be related. So the reductionist is at least obliged to give some account of these seeming intuitions or perceptions in terms which he finds acceptable; in terms of what are, from his point of view, respectable objects. Such objects will include (1) sentences themselves—not, of course, type-sentences, which are themselves abstract objects, but token-sentences, recognizably similar physical occurrences of visible and audible objects; (2) patterns of acceptance- or rejection-behavior, in relation to sentences or combinations of sentences, on the part of speakers and hearers; and, perhaps, if he is not too hard-line a materialist or behaviorist, (3) some avowedly mental phenomena such as feelings, images, sensations. The question is whether a plausible reduction of intuitions of conceptual necessity can be effected in such terms.

So we see that a complex obligation lies on the rejectionist. We must not make the obligation seem heavier than it is. The reductionist is not obliged to question the propriety or correctness of saying, for example, that someone has mastered a certain concept when he makes a correct use or application of a certain word in a variety of contexts, or of saying that a certain word signifies a certain property or that the possession of a certain property necessarily involves the possession of some other. What he will take himself to be objecting to is some theoretical picture which may sometimes accompany such remarks and may be supposed to explain their correctness or legitimacy, but which in fact explains nothing and *is* nothing but a philosophical fantasy. There may be a variety of such pictures: one may be that of people somehow becoming acquainted with abstract objects or concepts, associating them with other abstract objects (word-types) and then being governed or guided in their linguistic practice by their acquaintance with these abstract objects and by their ability to discern the relations in which they stand to one another (discernment of necessary truths) and to particular items which exemplify them in the world (correct empirical applications). Or there may be variant pictures with equally strong "mentalistic" tones. The rejectionist's task, as he sees it, must be to replace such pictures with an account of the natural realities which underlie and legitimize, or give sense to, those perfectly acceptable ways of talking about meanings, concepts, necessities, etc. which I have mentioned.

2. A NATURALISTIC REDUCTION: CORRECTNESS, AND AGREEMENT, IN USE

The most powerful and influential attempt on this task is due to the later Wittgenstein, the Wittgenstein of the *Philosophical Investigations*. It can be summed up in the famous equation of *meaning* and *use*. But the summary needs some expansion. Consider the case of somebody learning the meaning of a particular common word or, simply, coming to know what the word means. The followers of Wittgenstein are apt to speak of a preliminary period of *training* in the use (or meaning) of the word; though this may seem a rather inappropriately military-sounding description of the learning process, which is usually, I take it, a less regimented affair than this—more a matter of picking it up, with, perhaps, some occasional correction. But we need not bother about that. The point is that after a time the learner comes to find it *utterly natural* to make a certain application of the expression; he comes to apply it in a certain way *as a matter of course*. (These are Wittgenstein's phrases.) Here we may see one of the suspect pictures being, as it were, undermined or deflated: viz. the picture of the learner's application of the word being governed by, or determined by, his acquired acquaintance with the abstract thing, its sense or *meaning*, or the universal *property* or whatnot which he means by it—a kind of abstract standard serving as a check or guide to which he can make mental reference whenever he needs to. All this, it is suggested, is quite empty and gratuitous; all that happens is that, after a time, the learner just finds it *utterly natural* to use the expression in a certain way; he does so *as a matter of course*.

Now evidently, the fact that someone finds it utterly natural to proceed in a certain way does not necessarily mean, is no guarantee, that he is proceeding in the right way. If we are to associate meaning so closely with use, we must at least insist that the association is with *correct* use. But if we advert only to how the learner or speaker finds it natural to use the expression, what applications of it he finds it natural to make, the notion of correct use seems to be left out of account altogether. Or, worse, if we try to bring it in by identifying "correct use" with "use he finds it natural to make," we are abolishing the distinction between "correct" and "seems to him correct"; and that is tantamount to destroying the notion of correctness altogether, depriving us of the right to speak of corrrectness.

Of course, Wittgenstein has his answer ready to this. Indeed, if construed as an objection, it would be playing into his hands; for it is in fact a variant on one of his own arguments. There must indeed, he agrees, be a place for the idea of correct use. And there is such a place. There is such a place because language is essentially a social phenomenon. We are not dealing— indeed the above argument suggests we could not be dealing— with isolated individual language-users. We are dealing with communities of language-users. And the test of correctness of use of an expression is the test of conformity—or failure of conformity—with the agreed common practice in the use of the expression in a given community. And for this to be a test, in the case of expressions applicable to what happens in nature, there must be shared or sharable access to circumstances in which members of the speech-community by and large agree in the application of the expression; i.e. there must be publicly observable bases for the application of such expressions. It is these which Wittgenstein calls "criteria." Hence the famous doctrine that inner processes stand in need of outward criteria. (The argument about inner processes and outward criteria, sensation-language and so on can be seen, as Kripke has pointed out,[2] as a consequence of the more general considerations to the effect that grasp of meanings, following a meaning-rule, etc., is a matter of agreeing in a common linguistic practice, a matter, as Wittgenstein puts it, of sharing in a common "form of life.")

Similar considerations will apply, on this view, where it is not a matter of empirical application of an expression to objects or events in the world, but a matter of necessary truth or necessary consequence, of calculation, of what follows logically from what, of what is recognized as a demonstrative proof and so on. Here again there is rough general agreement in practice, readiness to agree on what is a mistake, etc., a shared form of life; and anyone who shares in this form of life, who has acquired in these respects the same disposition as other members of the speech-community, is said to have mastered the relevant concepts or operations.

The great point, on this view of the matter, is that there is,

---

2. S. Kripke, *Wittgenstein on Rules and Private Language* (London: Oxford, 1982).

philosophically speaking, nothing behind all this, and no need for anything beyond or behind it all to constitute a philosophical explanation of it. This is not to say that there are not biological and anthropological and cultural-historical explanations of how speech-communities agreeing in common linguistic practices came about. Such explanations there may well be. But as far as the philosophical problem is concerned, the suggestion is that we can just rest with, or take as primitive, the great natural fact that we *do* form speech-communities, agree in linguistic practice, and so on; that we have, if you will, a natural disposition to develop the dispositions which qualify us for such a description, the description, namely, "members of a speech-community, agreeing in a common linguistic practice." The great natural fact *covers* the phenomena. It is unnecessary and misleading to appeal to abstract objects of thought and intensional relations (e.g. of entailment and incompatibility) between such objects, relations which we are supposed to be capable of grasping in thought. At best such talk is an attempt to do justice to some aspects of the phenomenology of thought; but a misleading attempt in so far as it appears to invoke objects and relations which have no place in the natural world, the only world there is.

So there is an outline (filled in with much more force and subtlety by Wittgenstein himself) of a purely naturalistic account, a naturalistic reduction, one might say, of *the matter of meaning*—and all that goes with it. But of course we must ask whether the account really does cover the phenomena—all the phenomena. Can it really do justice to our experience? to our experience, for example, of recognizing particular things as of a certain general character or kind? Can it really do justice, to echo the phrase used just now, to the phenomenology of thought? Can it even—to parody itself—do justice to the way in which we *agree in finding it natural to talk* about our experience, our thinking and our talk itself?

I have to confess to not seeing my way at all clearly here. All I can produce are remarks which may point in one direction or another. So what follows is a kind of inconclusive debate.

First, let us consider again the view that whatever exists at all exists in nature, in the world of objects, occurrences, processes in space-time; so that to talk of abstract objects, intensions, universals, meanings, etc. must either be to talk in an oblique way about things and happenings in nature and nothing over and above such things and happenings or be simply myth-making, indulging in fiction. This might look like a prejudice in the strict sense, a prejudgment of the issue. But it has more weight than that. For it is true of the happy Platonist, or in general of one who wants to regard talk of abstract entities, etc. as not simply an oblique way of talking of natural objects and happenings, that he finds it difficult to avoid, or is even happy to employ, idioms which belong primarily to our talk of natural things. He is apt to talk of his supposed non-natural things and their relations on analogy with talk of natural things and their relations and thereby to expose himself to the charge that his non-natural entities are pseudo-natural entities, i.e. pseudo-entities; that he is just dreaming up a pseudo-world as the myth-maker does or the writer of fiction. So the first constraint, or one of the first constraints, on the believer in abstract objects must be to avoid any suggestion that they are in any way like natural objects, to avoid any natural model for his objects and their relations. This he may find difficult; perhaps insuperably difficult.

So the reply to the objection to the naturalist reduction, that it rests on a prejudgment of the issue, is that it may do so—or it may not. The objection is neither upheld nor overruled.

Another objection that might be made to the Wittgensteinian picture of the matter of meaning, as I roughly drew it,[3] might be that it yields a purely external view of the matter, a behaviorist view; and that it thereby neglects altogether the inner experience of understanding what you say or what is said, of seeing that one thing follows from another and so on. But as a reading of the *Investigations* will quickly show, Wittgenstein does not neglect these things at all. He is perfectly ready to acknowledge such an inner experience as, say, that of grasping the meaning of a formula or of meaning something by a word. But he asks what makes it right to describe an experience in this way. And the answer resides in the use the subject makes of the expression, the application he makes of it—let the experience be what it may. So the second objection, at least as stated, cannot be upheld either.

3. THE DEBATE OVER RECOGNITION

It may be, however, that these objections were incompletely stated or not stated in the right way. Let us go back to the two key notions in the Wittgensteinian picture of the matter of meaning:

(1) First, we have the notion of the speaker who has learned the meaning of an expression finding it *utterly natural* to apply

---

3. Here, as elsewhere, the phrase "Wittgensteinian picture" and similar expressions must be construed as meaning "picture or view suggested by Wittgenstein's writings." I am not rash enough to claim to have captured his exact intentions—or those of his interpreters.

it in a certain way, to make certain applications of it; he does so *as a matter of course*. This replaces the picture of his being guided by his knowledge or grasp of the abstract thing, the meaning or the concept or the universal (or the meaning-rule).

(2) Second, we have the elucidation of the notion of *correctness* of use or application in terms of *common agreement in linguistic practice*, a shared form of life. And it is an important point here that the fact of agreement in practice should be observable, should be something *publicly observable*. This is a necessary condition of its providing a criterion of correctness, a justification of saying that an expression is used correctly.

Consider the first of these notions in connection with one of the simplest types of case of the use of an expression: the application of a descriptive general term or predicate to an observed natural object. Certainly we do find it utterly natural to describe or refer to such a thing as, say, "red in color" or as "a car." Certainly we do so as a matter of course. But what does this mean and why is this so? It isn't just that, after a period of training or conditioning, the words come bubbling out of our mouths when we are confronted with a red object or a car; as a dog, after conditioning, might salivate at the sound of a bell. Roughly speaking, we say what we say because we recognize what we see. We see what we see *as* red or *as* a car. If we are to be true to our experience, we cannot elide or pass over the experience of recognition, of *seeing as*. Wittgenstein, in part II of the *Investigations*, though in a rather limited context, has much to say of the experience of *seeing as*. Some of the things he says, some of the phrases he uses or toys with, are of particular interest in the present connection. Thus he says: "The flashing of an aspect on us [i.e. suddenly seeing something as such-and-such] seems half visual experience, half thought."[4] He asks: "is it a case of both seeing and thinking? or an *amalgam* of the two, as I should almost like to say?"[5] Again, he has the phrase, " 'the echo of a thought in sight' one would like to say."[6] Elsewhere I have myself suggested some variant metaphors such as: the visual experience is "infused with" or "irradiated by" or "soaked with" *the concept.*[7] Finally, one more phrase of Wittgenstein's: "What I perceive in the dawning of an aspect [i.e. in coming to see something as something] . . . is an internal relation between it [the object] and other objects."[8]

Metaphor apart, what have we here? Well, we have an attempt to characterize what is undoubtedly a type of natural happening, a subjective experience, something that occurs in nature, the instantaneous recognition or seeing of something *as* such-and-such or *as* a so-and-so. The experience, the particular subjective happening, occurs in a moment, is instantaneous, is exhausted in the moment of its occurrence. And yet it seems that it cannot be exhaustively or veridically characterized without reference to what is not contained in the moment or in any moment, what is intrinsically general, the concept or abstract idea which the object seen is seen as an instance of and which other objects not then seen can be instances of as well. So, at least, one may be tempted to gloss Wittgenstein's remarks that a thought is echoed in the sight and that what one perceives is an internal relation between the object seen and other objects.

---

4. Wittgenstein, *Investigations*, part II, trans. Anscombe (Oxford: Blackwell), p. 197.
5. *Ibid.*
6. *Ibid.*, p. 212.
7. Strawson, "Imagination and Perception," in *Freedom and Resentment* (London: Methuen, 1974), p. 57.
8. Wittgenstein, *Investigations*, p. 212.

Seeing-as involves *thinking-of-as* and thinking of as "internally related to" other objects of actual or possible perception, not now perceived; and what does "thinking of as internally related to . . ." mean here but "thinking of as falling under the same concept as, exemplifying the same universal as . . . "? So, we might be tempted to conclude, the bare commonplace fact of *perceptual recognition* contains implicitly the thought of the abstract general thing, the concept or universal; and hence contains implicitly the capacity to distinguish in thought between the particular objects in nature which exemplify the general types or characters on the one hand and the general types of characters which they exemplify on the other; and hence to *think* of the latter (objects not of perception but of thought alone) abstractly. Then theoretical recognition of concepts of universals as objects of thought alone would not appear as an explanatory hypothesis of dubious coherence but as the barest commonplace, as the mere acknowledgement of something implicit in our commonest and most evident experience (Platonism demystified).

So, I say, we might be tempted to conclude. But, of course, it is not a temptation which the reductive naturalist is likely to feel or to yield to. He may be ready enough to concede that perceiving involves perceiving-as, which involves thinking-of-as— or, as Wittgenstein puts it, that "the thought is echoed in the sight"; even that the veridical characterization of the momentary perception involves a reference beyond itself, to what is not contained in the moment; but he will be inclined to construe this further reference as a reference to the subject's disposition to behave in a certain way in relation to the object perceived, i.e. to treat it in a certain way and, especially, to speak of it or describe it in a certain way. Equally, of course, his opponent, the believer in intensions, will see this reaction as a missing of the point, a yielding to the reductionist pressure to recognize the existence of nothing which is not a natural object or episode.

Let us turn, then, to the second key notion in the Wittgensteinian picture: the notion of the criterion of the correct use of an expression being to be found in observable agreement in linguistic practice. Clearly this requires the possibility (and fact) of our recognizing that the *same* thing is being said in the *same* type of situation, the recognition of identity of *type* over differences of case; not only of situation-type, but of expression- or sentence-type. Here we seem to reach rock-bottom. To deny the reality or possibility of such recognition would, on the theory's own terms, be to deny the existence of any justification or basis for saying that a use of an expression was correct. So it would, on the theory's own terms, be giving up the attempt to elucidate the matter of meaning altogether. But to admit it seems to be admitting that we work, and must work, with the idea of general types which are, or may be, exemplified again and again in different particular instances; and such a general type is precisely the abstract thing which the anti-reductionist is contending we must admit the existence of.

As indicated earlier, it is important for the anti-reductionist to stress the point that he is not claiming to have discovered anything in the world which the reductionist has overlooked or denied. He is just calling attention to the platitude which assumes a particular prominence in the Wittgensteinian's own theory of meaning, resting as it does on the idea of observable agreement in linguistic practice: viz. the existence of the power, and of the exercise of the power, of recognizing particular things, including expression-utterances, as different instances of an identical type; but he is not saying that the identical type of which they are recognized as instances is an extra mysterious something in the world; for it is not in the world at all. It has no place, no date, no causal powers; it cannot be encountered in perception; only its instances, if any, can be so encountered. It is only in thought that it can be distinguished from its instances. So—if it exists at all—it is an object of thought alone.

The reductionist—the nominalist we may perhaps here call him—is, of course, not silenced. He will turn that last remark around. The abstract thing (universal, concept, type) is an object of thought alone? That is to say, it exists, if at all, only *as* an object of thought. But thought, thinking, is certainly a natural process, something that takes place in nature, has causes and effects. But however carefully we examine the processes of thought, of thinking, whether as neuroscientists or as introspective psychologists, we shall find nothing but natural items, events, or processes. We may, for example, find subvocally uttered or imaged tokens of symbols or sentences; but we shan't find types of which they are tokens or concepts which they signify or any other abstract entities. However, this riposte couples with the fault of *ignoratio elenchi* an equally evident defect. It embodies a confusion between being an object of thought (being what is thought about) and being a neural or mental constituent of the process of thinking. But evidently these are quite distinct; and we do not have to turn to abstract objects to see that they are. To say that some particular natural object, say Socrates, is the object of my thought—that I am thinking about Socrates—is not to say that that object is temporarily located in my brain or is an element in the stream of images, feelings, subvocal speech, or whatnot that makes up the content of my consciousness. And as with particular, natural objects, so with abstract objects—*if* such exist and *are* thought about.

4. THE DEBATE OVER NECESSITY

The discussion has so far been conducted largely on ground which might be thought relatively favorable to the reductionist, in that it has concerned mainly the empirical application of expressions to natural objects and the empirical tests for correctness of use. But there is also abstract and general thinking which at least appears to concern itself directly with concepts or universals, as in philosophy itself, or with other abstract objects, as in mathematics. In the expression of such thought, though not there alone, there is a marked tendency to employ the apparatus of reference, apparently in relation to such items: i.e. nominal expressions which appear to stand for such items or variables of quantification which appear to range over them. No proposal for eliminating such apparent reference ever looks faintly realistic. So one test of ontological commitment, a test favored by some nominalistically inclined philosophers, seems to put their nominalism at risk. Perhaps that does not matter; they may be ready to sacrifice the test to save their metaphysics. The real question, it may be said, is whether the recognition that such thinking—abstract thinking—occurs (and this is not denied) involves the theoretical recognition of abstract entities as objects of such thinking. And here some by now familiar moves are available to the reductive naturalist.

Whatever such thinking may experientially be like, he may argue, whatever mental contents it involves, the real test of its actually being the thinking of this or that thought, or indeed of anything at all, lies in what emerges from it; particularly in the way of speech or writing or, perhaps, the drawing of diagrams. Suppose a man claims that, by dint of hard abstract thinking, he has hit upon a conceptual truth or solved a problem or discovered a mathematical proof. Then see what sentences he actually produces as truth, solution, or proof and observe the reaction of his fellows (his peers). There are various possibilities of reaction. They may find it utterly natural to agree at once, or after some study; they may enter into detailed debate or suggest alterations or modifications or they may feel utterly blank and uncomprehending. Or there may be debate followed by agreement. And so on. Debate reactions, no less than agreement reactions, indicate what Wittgenstein would call a shared form of life, the common membership of a linguistic community. Blank incomprehension indicates a limit to, or a limited breakdown of, community. But this is all. There is no need to go further. The invoking of abstract thought has not really brought us on to new debating ground.

Evidently this reductionist response will not convince or satisfy the believer in concepts, universals, abstract entities. Consider, not simply the special case of what is held to be a new discovery, but the general case of what is represented as conceptual truth or mathematical truth or necessity; and of what, in this region, is generally accepted or believed or agreed on, or comes without difficulty to be generally accepted or believed or agreed on. According to the reductionist picture, as so far sketched, the natural fact of general acceptance or agreement is the only ultimate fact of the matter. It arises from our biologically and culturally formed disposition to share in a form of life of which such general agreement is a part. And that is all there is. There is, strictly speaking, no such extra or additional thing as the objective mathematical or conceptual truth or fact expressed in the agreed or accepted form of words. We may indeed speak of recognizing the validity of a proof or perceiving or grasping a conceptual connection; but such talk is just a reflection of our having learned a practice and finding it utterly natural to proceed in accordance with it.

Against all this the reductionist's opponent will protest that it is an unacceptable kind of collectivist subjectivism; that though our biological and cultural formation enters into our capacity to formulate and grasp conceptual and mathematical truths, those truths or facts themselves are no *more* dependent on our biologically and culturally formed human nature than are natural facts, facts about empirically encounterable objects. To think otherwise is altogether too casual a dismissal of that whole tradition which recognizes the power of reason (of "rational intuition") in relation to concepts or abstract objects of thought generally; which recognizes that such objects characteristically belong to systems of which the members stand to each other in logical relations accessible to rational insight and calculation.

At this point, however, it might be said that the two types of view here opposed to each other by no means exhaust the possibilities. For it is possible to reject the collectivist subjectivism which one party attributes to the Wittgensteinians without embracing that party's belief in a distinctive species of truth, necessary or conceptual truth, guaranteed by reason (or meaning) alone. This is precisely what Quine, in contrast with Wittgenstein, does, famously protesting that no proposition is so guaranteed, none is in principle immune from refutation in the course of experience. All the propositions (or, as he would say, sentences) which we accept as true relate, directly or indirectly, to the natural world, the only world there is, and all are answerable to our experience of that world. Very roughly speaking, all propositions are empirical. Those we are tempted to classify as non-empirical, as necessary, as guaranteed by reason or meaning alone, are simply more deeply rooted in our system of belief than others. They are more difficult to dislodge than others; but none is in principle undislodgeable. Any proposition can be given up, any can be preserved—just so long as we are prepared to make such adjustments elsewhere as are required to secure consistency in our system of beliefs. Since there is, on this view, no distinctive class of analytic or conceptually necessary truths, there is no argument from the existence of such truths to the existence of a class of abstract objects (objects of thought alone) which they are truths about.

It is fairly obvious where the breach can be made in the walls of this doctrine. It is at the point where the proviso is made about preserving consistency in the total system of beliefs. What is this that is to be, that must be, preserved? Why should the acceptance of one sentence or proposition entail the rejection or giving up of another? Why should there be any limitations at all on admissible combinations of beliefs—or of accepted sentences? The natural answer is: because it is absolutely (logically or conceptually) *impossible* that certain propositions should be jointly true. But this is to say that their conjunction is necessarily false; or, in other words, that the negation of their conjunction is necessarily true. So either we must give up the proviso about preserving consistency or we must accept necessary truth as a distinctive kind of truth. But to give up the proviso is to abandon rationality altogether.

There is another answer, however; and, curiously and interestingly enough, it returns us to the Wittgensteinian position to which the Quinian presented itself as an alternative or at least returns us to something very close to the Wittgensteinian position. It goes something like this. What is called the need to preserve consistency; the compulsion to give up some propositions on accepting others; the limitation on acceptable combinations of propositions—all these do indeed exist; but they exist simply as matters of natural (psychological and social) fact about the members of a community who share a common language, i.e. participate in a common form of life. It is a part of that participation that they naturally agree, or can be brought to agree, in rejecting certain combinations of propositions as, as they say, "inconsistent," or in accepting certain arguments as, as they say, "valid." But there is no need to look beyond these natural facts; there is nothing beyond to look to.

Some of the objections to this fallback Wittgensteinian position have already been rehearsed. But there is another objection, though it is one which the Wittgensteinian will dismiss impatiently enough. The objection is not that the Wittgensteinian description of the situation is untrue in its positive content. At its own level, and as far as it goes, it is true enough. There are these observable patterns of acceptance- and rejection-behavior on the part of language-users in relation to combinations of sentences. There is this observable convergence in agreement on the part of those trained or skilled in relevant disciplines or areas of thought and discourse. And, from a certain point of view, it is true that when such patterns of behavior have been noted and described, there is no more to be said. But this point of view is, so to speak, an externalist point of view, which we can perhaps adopt for part of the time, but which we cannot occupy consistently and all the time. For we are not merely observers of language-use on the part of others, not merely observers of the linguistic manifestations of the thought of others. We are thinkers and language-users ourselves; and indeed it is only because we have *this* role that we can follow with understanding the linguistic practice of others. As thinkers and speakers ourselves, confronted with the claim that the Wittgensteinian picture exhausts the phenomena, says all there is to say, we may well find the claim impossible to believe, may well be tempted to say that it simply is not true to our most evident experience; for, we may be tempted to say, we do not merely experience compulsions, merely find it natural to say, in general, what (we can observe that) others say too, or to agree with this or to question that; rather, we understand the meaning of what we say and hear well enough to be able, sometimes at least, to recognize, in what is said, inconsistencies and consequences which are attributable solely to the sense or meaning of what is said; to grasp, in effect, the propositions expressed by the words uttered in the context of their utterance. To put the point in old-fashioned language, we do naturally claim the power to discern "relations of ideas," as Hume would put it (i.e. relations of incompatibility, entailment, or equivalence); or, as Descartes would say, the power of "clear and distinct perception" of necessary truths; or, as both he and Spinoza would say, the power of "rational intuition" of such truths.

If this very natural reaction is correct, if these claims are justified, then the supposedly suspect terminology of meanings, concepts, types, attributes, universals, and abstract objects generally; of propositions or thoughts (in Frege's sense); of necessary or conceptual truths guaranteed by meaning alone—all this is in order as it stands, without need or possibility of reduction; and the free use we appear to make of the apparatus of reference to such abstract entities is a natural and legitimate reflection of the fact.

It would be tedious to go once again at length over the reductive naturalist's reaction to this reaction. He will, of course, be ready enough to acknowledge the psychological reality of the experiences, the mental occurrences, which we are inclined to report in the idiom of rational intuition, the idiom of seeing or perceiving necessary connections between concepts, or grasping truths of reason, or whatnot. For thinking is a natural phenomenon and these psychological events, whatever account is given of them, are genuine events in nature. He may even allow that the idioms in which we are prone to describe them embody a natural, even a laudable, attempt to hit off their distinctive character. But there he must draw the line. However natural we find this attempt to do justice to the phenomenology of thought, he will say it is a misguided attempt in so far as it appears to invoke objects (and a power of intuitive apprehension of those objects) which have no place in this, the natural, and the only world; and hence falls into myth.

5. SOLUTION OR CONFLICT? AN INCONCLUSIVE CONCLUSION

It is not my purpose to come down finally on one side or the other of this prolonged debate over an issue which, in one form or another, is likely to provide philosophers with matter for argument as long as there are philosophers left to argue. But it is my purpose to suggest a resemblance between this case and some of those others considered earlier. As in those cases, it seems possible to distinguish two standpoints from which the phenomena in question can be viewed: the phenomena, in this case, of thought, experience, and language (inseparable as these are, at any developed level, from each other). We can view the phenomena from the externalist or strictly or reductively naturalist standpoint from which nothing is to be acknowledged as real which we cannot, as it were, place in nature; or we can view them from the inside, as speakers and thinkers ourselves, who sometimes at least appear to ourselves to have as objects of our thought, not only natural objects and events, but the general and the abstract, concepts or ideas or universals, objects exemplifiable, but not locatable, in nature; and, moreover, whose most common experience (recognition) of natural objects and events appears implicitly to provide for the possibility of such thought. Both standpoints are in a sense natural to us. Let us call them, for convenience, by old names: (1) the nominalist and (2) the realist standpoints. The naturalness of the second, or realist, standpoint is attested both by an old philosophical tradition and by our free use of what at least appears on the surface to be the apparatus of reference to abstract objects. It has its roots in the *experience* of thought and of recognition. The naturalness of the first, or nominalist, standpoint is attested by its predominance in the current climate of philosophical thought and by the difficulty which realists often experience in avoiding analogies with natural objects and relations in speaking of abstract objects and their relations to each other and to natural objects. It has *its* roots in the strong natural disposition, which I have frequently alluded to, to understand by the notion of existence the same thing as existence in nature; to think that whatever exists at all exists in nature. And this disposition no doubt has its roots in the fact—grateful to Marxist ears, though not to them alone—that thought is fundamentally, for us, at the service of action or practice; and what in practice or action we have to deal with are, as we ourselves are, natural objects and events.

In previous cases, I have suggested that a reconciliation of apparently conflicting views could be achieved by relativizing the conception of the real, of what really exists or is really the case, to different standpoints, acknowledging that a man can occupy one standpoint without rationally debarring himself from occupying the other. Applied to the present case, this would yield the result that, from the standpoint of strict naturalism, all that is real, all that there really is in the region we are concerned with, is the range of natural phenomena which can be exhaustively described in Wittgensteinian or Quinian-Wittgensteinian terms; while, from the other standpoint, that of non-reductive or catholic naturalism, the notion of existence in this region is extended to include what we so readily speak of, or appear to speak of, viz. thought-objects, not locatable in nature, though sometimes exemplified there.

I must confess, however, that in this case I think such a solution is less likely to be found satisfactory than the corresponding move may be found, and I think ought to be found, in the earlier cases. I think it more likely that one party will continue to find the other the victims of self-indulgent illusion, while the second party finds the first the slaves of narrow prejudice. For this reason, if for no other, I am less satisfied with such a solution myself.

If the conflict is irreconcilable and I have to declare an allegiance—or, better, a sympathy—it lies with the realists or catholic naturalists rather than with the nominalists or strict naturalists. And that will perhaps have been evident.

The strong nominalist will say, of his opponent, in Wittgenstein's famous phrase, that "a picture holds him captive." To the strong realist, on the other hand, it will appear that his opponent is in the grip of a reductive rage, a rage to reduce thought; and he will find it noteworthy, and ironical, that this reductive rage is perhaps most common today among the most scrupulous thinkers.

I prefaced these chapters with an epigraph from Gibbon. I should like to end them with another·observation by that enlightened historian:

Philosophy alone can boast (and perhaps it is no more than the boast of philosophy) that her gentle hand is able to eradicate from the human mind the latent and deadly principle of fanaticism.

Index